100 Stories
of
Hadhrat Ayesha رضي الله عنها

كَانَتْ عَائِشَةُ اَفْقَهَ النَّاسِ وَ اَعْلَمَ النَّاسِ
وَ اَحْسَنَ النَّاسِ رَأْيًا فِي الْعَامِةِ

100 Stories

of

Hadhrat Ayesha رضی اللہ عنہا

By:

Moulana Shuaib Saror

Translation Edited By:

Mufti Afzal Hoosen Elias

(May Allaah Protect him)

ZAM ZAM
PUBLISHERS

*ZAM ZAM
PUBLISHERS*

Second Authorized Edition 2014

Title : **100 Stories of Hadhrat Ayesha** رضي الله عنها

By : Moulana Shuaib Saror

Translated By : Mufti Afzal Hoosen Elias (May Allaah Protect him)

Second Published May 2014

Published By:

Zam Zam Publishers

Urdu Bazar Karachi-Pakistan.
Ph : 0092-21-32760374
0092-21-32761671
Fax : 0092-21-32761673
E-mail : zamzampublisher@gmail.com

http://www.

www.zamzampublishers.com

Books Also Available in :

United Kingdom

AL-FAROOQ-INTERNATIONAL
Leicester

AZHAR ACADEMY LTD.
London E12 5QA

ISLAMIC BOOK CENTER
Bolton Bl1 3NE

U.S.A

ZEENAT EMPORIUM
Chicago

South Africa

AL-HUDA PUBLICATIONS
Johannesburg

Contents

Introduction

All praise belongs to Allaah, we laud Him, seek His assistance and from Him only do we seek forgiveness. We bring Imaan in Him and solely rely on Him. We seek Allaah's protection from the evil of ourselves and our actions. Whoever Allaah guides can never be led astray and whoever He leads astray can never be guided. We bear witness that there is none worthy of worship but Allaah and that our leader, intercessor and master Muhammed ﷺ is his servant and Rasul. We seek Allaah's protection from Shaytaan the accursed. In the name of Allaah the Most Gracious Most Merciful.

"For Muslim men and Muslim women, Mu'mineen men and Mu'mineen women, obedient men and obedient women, truthful men and truthful women, men who exercise Sabr and women who exercise Sabr, humble men and humble women, charitable men and charitable women, fasting men and fasting women, chaste men and chaste women, and men who remember Allaah in abundance and women who remember Allaah; Allaah has prepared forgiveness and an immense reward for *(all of)* them."*(Surah Ahzaab: 35)*

The Deen of Islaam is the religion of truth and the true Deen. It protects the rights of man and guides man in every aspect of humanlife. It removed man from the filth it was drowning in and guided man to the straight path. The light of Tauheed removed the darkness of Kufr and Shirk as well as the other vices in society such as oppression, murder, theft, injustice, hatred, lewdness, immorality, deceit were all removed and replaced it with shame, modesty, justice, security, love and mercy.

Whenever Islaam spread the light of its noble teachings, the success and elevation of that society cannot be denied by anyone.

When one studies the other religions of the world then one would never find any woman attaining a lofty position in that religion, even if she were to sacrifice her life for it. However Islaam is that religion of truth which elevated the position and status of woman at every juncture.

Islaam awarded women honour as mothers, daughters, sisters and as wives and those women who were blessed with becoming the honourable wives of Rasulullaah ﷺ they were awarded the status of becoming the mothers of the entire Ummat.

The Noble Quraan and blessed Hadeeth of Rasulullaah ﷺ have enumerated the illustrious virtue in numerous places. However the virtues which have been mentioned regarding Hadhrat Aisha ﵂ surpass all those which have been mentioned for the other wives of Rasulullaah ﷺ. There are many reasons for these numerous virtues and her lofty rank. In addition to being in the wedlock of Rasulullaah ﷺ, she was a perfect and sterling example of how to lead a correct lifestyle. Her life story is a perfect guide on how women of Islaam should lead their lives; What qualities they should instil within themselves, how should their married lives be, what relationship they should have with their husbands, how should and in essence how they should live. In addition it teaches one the manner in which a woman can accomplish greatness in the fields of knowledge.

In short the life of Hadhrat Aisha ﵂ is the perfect handbook in all these aspects and in following in her footsteps one will most certainly attain the objective.

However it is indeed extremely distressing that very few women today who take lesson from the life of Hadhrat Aisha ﷺin how lead their lives. In fact the reality today is that imitating the habits and ideals of the west has become second nature of the Ummat today. It is plaguing the Ummat like a cancer and one fears that it might spread and ultimately destroy society completely.

Nevertheless in these trying times it is necessary to revive Islaamic scruples and principles in society. In order to achieve this it is incumbent to present the lives and noble personalities of the blessed women of this Ummat so that women of today can be inspired to follow in their footsteps.

The book before you, "Hundred stories of Hadhrat Aisha" has been prepared with this in mind, wherein the life and practices of Hadhrat Aisha ﷺhave been highlighted, which will assist one in leading a noble life. Whoever will use this book as a guide will undoubtedly find it useful in bettering one's life and strengthening one's Imaan.

Unique features of this book

1- This book has been prepared from reliable and authentic references of Tafseer, Hadeeth and history. The relevant references have also been cited.

2- Wherever further explanation was required, it was provided with reference to authentic interpretations.

3- At times page numbers were cited for the relevant books of Hadeeth.

4- The book begins with a brief biography of Hadhrat Aisha ﷺas well as some of the virtues mentioned regarding her in Hadeeth and by the senior scholars of the Ummat.

5- At times the subject matter was reinforced with relevant poetry, while each story was provided with an eye-catching title.

Gratitude and thanks

If those who assisted in the compilation and publication of this book are not mentioned then this will be a sign of ingratitude. At this juncture I would like to thank my mentor and guide Hadhrat Moulana Naazim Ashraf Sahib (the rector of Baitul Uloom), on whose instruction this work began and under whose guidance and with whose supplications this work was completed. May Allaah reward Hadhrat Moulana and all those who assisted him with a gracious reward. May Allaah Ta'ala increase them in their knowledge and practise. Aameen

Lastly I appeal to the readers; I admit to my deficiency in knowledge and lack of ability and since this work was the result of limited research it has most definitely not done justice to the topic. Therefore if the reader finds any benefit in this book then it is solely from Allaah and the fruits of the supplications of my seniors but if any error is found in it then it is from Shaytaan and a result of my own weakness.

We ask Allaah to accept this small effort in His court, make it a means of benefit for all, and a means of salvation for myself, my parents and teachers. *Aameen*

Muhammed Shuaib Saror

بسم الله الرحمن الرحيم

Name and lineage

Her name is Aisha. Her title was Siddiqah and commonly called Umie Abdullaah and Ummul Mu'mineen. Her lineage from her father, Hadhrat Abu Bakr is as follows,

Aisha the daughter of Abu Bakr, who was the son of Abu Kuhaafah, the son of Uthmaan, the son of Aamir, the son of Umar, the son of Ka'ab, the son of Sa'ad, the son of Teem, the son of Murrah, the son of Ka'ab, the son of Lu'ay, the son of Ghaalib, the son of Fahr, the son of Maalik.

Her lineage from her mother, Hadhrat Umie Rumaan is as follows,

Aisha the daughter of Umie Rumaan, who was the daughter of Aamir, the son Aamir, the son of Uwaimir, the son of Abdus Shams, the son of Ataab, the son of Uthniyah, the son of Sabee'a, the son of Dahmaan, the son of Haarith, the son of Ghatam, the son of Maalik, the son of Kinaanah.

Hadhrat Aisha's foster mother was the wife of Waa'il.

The lineage of Hadhrat Aisha from her father's side meets with that of Rasulullaah in the seventh generation and from her mother's side in the eleventh and twelfth generation. Her father, Hadhrat Abu Bakr was the first amongst the men to embrace Islaam and was the companion of Rasulullaah's even before embracing Islaam and after. The virtues, merits, status and piety of Hadhrat Abu Bakr are impossible to deny. In a similar manner her mother, Hadhrat Umie Rumaan ﷺ was also amongst the esteemed and revered Sahabiyaat of Rasulullaah ﷺ.

Birth

Hadhrat Umie Rumaan was first married to Abdullaah Azdie. After the demise of Abdullaah Azdie, Hadhrat Abu Bakr ﷺ proposed and married her. She granted Hadhrat Abu Bakr ﷺ a son, Abdur Rahmaan ﷺ, and a daughter, Hadhrat Aisha ﷺ.

Her exact date of birth is not mentioned in the books of history. However it has been established that three years prior to Hijrat she was six years old. She was six years old when her Nikaah was performed to Rasulullaah ﷺ and in Shawwaal 1 A.H, at the age of nine; she went to live with Rasulullaah ﷺ. At the age of eighteen, 11 Rabi'ul Awwal 11 A.H she became widow. In this manner her date of birth has been ascertained to be the end of the fifth year of Nabuwwat, that is Shawwaal nine years prior to Hijrat, corresponding to the English date July 614 C.E.

Childhood

The Mother of the believers, beloved of the beloved of Allaah, Hadhrat Aisha Siddiqah ﷺ opened her eyes in the home of the Siddeeq ﷺ, which was the first to be radiated and rejuvenated with the beauty of Islaam. Kufr and Shirk would never dare to even glance at the home which was the first to be illuminated with the light of Nabuwwat. This is the reason why Hadhrat Aisha ﷺ is amongst those fortunate and revered individuals who remained pure and unscathed from the clutches of Kufr, Shirk, deviation and innovation.

Whenever Rasulullaah ﷺ would enter the home of Hadhrat Abu Bakr and recite Quraan in a soft and gentle manner in the Masjid in his home, Hadhrat Aisha would derive benefit from Rasulullaah ﷺ. Even though the age of childhood is but childhood, those individuals for whom Allaah Ta'ala has destined greatness are endowed with the aptitude and proficiency early in their lives. In this manner Hadhrat Aisha did not let her childhood pass without deriving benefit and through her remarkable memory made these days of childhood both constructive and valuable.

Her memory

She narrates then when the following verse was revealed,

"The fact is that Qiyaamah is their appointment *(with truly severe punishment)* and Qiyaamah shall be most severe and most bitter *(for them)*." *(Surah Qamar: 46)*

She was playing.

Similarly she relates that on one occasion she was playing with her toys, amongst which was a winged horse. When Rasulullaah ﷺ passed by he enquired about it, to which she replied that it was a horse. Rasulullaah ﷺ replied that horses do not have wings. Hadhrat Aisha said, "Why not? Did not the horse of Hadhrat Sulaimaan have wings?"[1]

---

[1] 'Mishkaat'

Education and reformation

Under the guidance of her father

Hadhrat Abu Bakr ﵁ raisedhis daughter and gave her a sturdy upbringing in the same manner as his other children, which continued even after her marriage. It is for this reason that she would fear the rebuke of her father when committing even the slightest error and Hadhrat Abu Bakr ﵁ at times would even reprimand her in the presence of Rasulullaah ﷺ.

Under the best of teachers

Even though Hadhrat Aisha ﵂received her primary and basic education from her father, her actual education and upbringing began after coming to live with Rasulullaah ﷺ as his wife.

Rasulullaah ﷺ is the teacher and guide for mankind, who saw to the reformation of every aspect of Hadhrat Aisha's ﵂ life. Wherever he saw some shortcoming then through his advice and teaching he would remove it. In addition to this it was the noble habit of Hadhrat Aisha ﵂that whenever she faced any difficulty or did not understand some aspect of Deen then she would immediately refer to Rasulullaah ﷺ. **It was during this time that she learned to read and write as well as learnt to recite the Quraan. She was also an expert with regards to Arab ancestry. She learnt the science of medicine from various Arab delegations. In addition to being well-versed and proficient with regards to the intricacies of Shari'ah, its laws and injunctions; she also possessed a unique proficiency in deriving laws from the Quraan and Sunnat.** In this manner the tutorage and direction of the best of teachers for all mankind proved to be the principle cause and reason for her attaining superiority in the both knowledge and virtue.

Homelife

Her life at home was one of simplicity, of scarcity and difficulty. The home in which she had come was the home of Nabuwwat, which possessed very little or almost no worldly possessions. It was difficult to even light the lamp and at times up to forty days would pass and a lamp would not be lit. Sometimes months would pass and a fire could not be lit. They would suffice with dry bread and water. Even if something were to come into the home then their generous nature was such that they would spend it in the path of Allaah. It was just Rasulullaah ﷺ and Hadhrat Aisha رضي الله عنها in the home and after sometime the slave, Hadhrat Bareerah رضي الله عنها also became part of this household.

At the same time this house was blessed with tremendous wealth and that was the love and affection of this house for each other. This is the reason that in the nine years she lived with Rasulullaah ﷺ there was no serious argument or dispute between them despite all the difficulty and hardship they endured. The fragrance of love, affection, care, concern and unity continued to emanate from their home.

Character and personality

Allaah Ta'ala has blessed Hadhrat Aisha رضي الله عنها with many praiseworthy and exemplary traits. Despite her life of difficulty and hardship she never once complained and remained content, always obeying Rasulullaah ﷺ and endeavouring to please him. She would even keep in mind the close relatives of Rasulullaah ﷺ.

Her devotion to Ibaadaat was such that she never missed performing her Tahajjud, Chaasht as well as other Nafl Ibaadaat. She would fast even on the most scorching days. She had the habit to perform Hajj every year (after the demise of Rasulullaah ﷺ). She was ever-fearful of Allaah Ta'ala and was always concerned over the Aakhirah. At times her concern for the Aakhirah would cause her to tear uncontrollably. She was extremely soft hearted. Her generosity and kind-heartedness was such that she gave a hundred thousand dirhams as Sadaqah in one day and would not keep a single dirham for herself. She would always come to the assistance of other women and would never fail to intercede on their behalf, in permissible matters.

Hadhrat Aisha ﷺ would never turn any person and to the best of her abilities would try to assist them. Even though she was gentle in nature she was just. Her bravery and courage was such that she would wake in the dead of the night and visit the graveyard on her own. Her services and exploits have left their mark on the ages of Islaamic conquest and she did not fear even the mightiest of governors. She was very considerate and took into account the smallest aspects when dealing with people. She always fulfilled the responsibility of calling towards good, preventing evil and reconciling between people. She was kind to her servants and those under her care. **She would maintain good relations even with the other wives of Rasulullaah ﷺ and would openly highlight their virtues and noble qualities. Treating people in the manner that they deserve was her second nature.**

Throughout her life she abstained from the evil habits of backbiting, slander, lying, cursing and seeking out the faults of others. **She strictly abided to the laws of Hijaab, which is the inherent quality of women, such that she wished to even observe Hijaab from her foster father until Rasulullaah ﷺ prevented her from doing so and she obeyed.**

Despite possessing such meritorious traits and virtues, Allaah Ta'ala endowed her with the qualities of humility and humbleness to such an extent that she even disliked hearing others praising her. This same quality remained with her to the end of her days and even on her death bed was apprehensive of allowing Hadhrat Abdullaah bin Abbaas to enter, fearing that he might begin praising her.

In essence her personality was assembly of attributes of nobility, possessing such outstanding traits such as truthfulness, piety, trustworthiness, contentment, obedience, purity, generosity, bravery, intelligence, helpfulness, devoutness, perception, eloquence, chastity, fear of Allaah, asceticism, simplicity, compassion, humility, patience, forgiving, as well as many other noble traits.

Narrations of Hadeeth

A great number of Sahabah and Sahabiyaat derived benefit from Hadhrat Aisha. In the same manner as other senior Sahabah, **Hadhrat Aisha also dictated the entire Quraan to her servant, Abu Yunus, who was able to read and write.** Numerous commentaries of Hadhrat Aisha on verses of the Noble Quraan have also been reported. The number of narrations in this regard can be estimated by the fact that of all the narrations which Imaam Muslim reported in 'Saheeh Muslim' in the chapter of Tafseer, majority are the narrations of Hadhrat Aisha and Hadhrat Abdullaah bin Abbaas.

She excelled in the field of Hadeeth as well and was a living example of the Hadeeth, "Narrate from me, even if it be one verse". She constantly imparted the teachings of Rasulullaah to the Ummat. **It is for this reason that the number of narrations reported from Hadhrat Aisha number 2210**

and is the most amount of Ahaadeeth reported, with the exception of a few.Of these narrations, 286 have been reported in 'Bukhaari' and 'Muslim' with 174 common between them. The other narrations can be found in the other books of Hadeeth[1].

Teaching

In addition to the numerous narrations reported by Hadhrat Aisha ﵂, Fiqh, Ijtihaad, and deriving Deeni rulings were a radiant page in the biography of Hadhrat Aisha ﵂. She not only surpassed all of the women in this Ummat but the men as well.

At the time when Hadhrat Ali ﵁moved the Islaamic capital to Kufah then the majority of the senior Sahabah were residing in other countries and towns, which resulted in the people of Madinah referring to those Sahabah who now remained in Madinah and even more to Hadhrat Aisha ﵂.

Later when the remaining Sahabah also left to spread the teachings of Islaam across the world, Hadhrat Aisha ﵂ still resided in Madinah. Young girls, women, and those men who were the blood relatives of Hadhrat Aisha ﵂would frequent her home to take lessons from her. They would sit in her home while she gave her discourses whilst others remained seated in the Masjid courtyard. A curtain would cover the door and from within the confines of her home she would instruct and teach the masses, answering their questions and religious rulings.

In addition to these educational discourses, many young boys and girls would come to her for religious instruction, as well as many orphans she had taken in her care. **In this manner every**

[1]'Seerat Aisha' page 188

year on Hajj, her tent would be erected between Hira and Thabeer and the Muslims of the world would surround her and derive benefit from the lessons she taught from her tent. It is for this reason that all of the senior scholars of the Taabi'een derived benefit from Hadhrat Aisha ﷺ.

Virtues and merits

Her status according to Allaah

What was the status of Hadhrat Aisha ﷺaccording to Allaah Ta'ala? One will easily be able to understand this by considering the following;

1- Allaah Ta'ala revealed seventeen verses testifying to the honour and chastity of Hadhrat Aisha ﷺ, which is a part of the Quraan and will always testify to her honour and chastity.

2- Allaah Ta'ala revealed the verse of Tayammum because of Hadhrat Aishaﷺ, creating ease for the entire Ummat.

3- Hadhrat Jibraeel ﷺ with the permission of Allaah came with a picture of Hadhrat Aisha ﷺ to Rasulullaah ﷺ informing him, "This will be your wife in this world and Aakhirah."

4- Similarly Rasulullaah ﷺ conveyed the salaam of Hadhrat Jibraeel ﷺto Hadhrat Aisha ﷺ,

" إنّ جبرئيل يقرأ عليك السلام "

"Indeed Jibraeel has conveyed Salaam upon you."[1]

[1] 'Bukhaari' , 'Muslim', 'Tirmidhi'

Her status in the eyes of Rasulullaah ﷺ

The status of Hadhrat Aisha رضي الله عنها in the eyes of Rasulullaah ﷺ is not hidden from anybody and is well-known to everybody.

5-

«عن ابى موسى الاشعرى قال قال النبى ﷺ فضل عائشة على النسآء كفضل الثريد على سائر الطعام -»

Hadhrat Abu Moosa Ash'ari رضي الله عنه narrates that Rasulullaah ﷺ said, "The superiority of Aisha over other women is like the superiority of Thareed[1] over all food."[2]

6-

«عن عمرو بن العاص ان النبى ﷺ بعثه على جيش ذات السلاسل فاتيته فقلت اى الناس احب اليك قال عائشة »

Hadhrat Amr bin Aas narrates that he asked Rasulullaah ﷺ who was most beloved to him and he replied, "Aisha."[3]

7- On one occasion Rasulullaah ﷺ said,

«لا توزينى فى عائشة فان الوحى لم يأتنى و أنا فى ثوب امراة الآ عائشة »

"Do not cause me pain with regards to Aisha because undoubtedly revelation does not descend upon me when I am on the bed of any person except Aisha."[4]

---

[1]A meal prepared by mixing gravy and bread.
[2]'Bukhaari', 'Muslim', 'Tirmidhi
[3]ibid
[4]ibid

8- On one occasion Rasulullaah ﷺ said to Hadhrat Fatima رضي الله عنها,

«اى بنيه الست تحبين ما احب فقالت بلى فقال فاحبى هذه لعائشة »

"O beloved daughter! Do you not love whom I love?" Hadhrat Fatima رضي الله عنها replied that she most certainly does, on which Rasulullaah ﷺ said, "Then love Aisha."[1]

9- Hadhrat Aisha رضي الله عنها was the person who chewed the miswaak for Rasulullaah ﷺ before giving it to him before his demise. When Rasulullaah ﷺ was in his final illness and was spending each day at the home of each of his wives, he kept asking whose turn it was awaiting the day when it would be Hadhrat Aisha's رضي الله عنها turn. After taking permission from all of his wives he later moved into the house of Hadhrat Aisha to spend the remainder of his days.

In the eyes of the scholars of the Ummat

10-

«عن ابى موسى قال ما اشكل علينا اصحاب رسول الله ﷺ حديث قط فسألنا عائشة الا وجدنا عندها منه علمًا »

Hadhrat Abu Moosa Ash'ari رضي الله عنه narrates, "Whenever we doubted any Hadeeth reported from Rasulullaah ﷺ, we would refer it to Hadhrat Aisha رضي الله عنها and we would find her to be knowledgeable of the Hadeeth."[2]

[1] Ibid
[2] 'Tirmidhi'

11-

«عن موسى طلة قال ما رأيت احدا افصح من عائشة »

Hadhrat Moosa bin Talha narrates, "I have not seen anyone more eloquent than Aisha رضي الله عنها."

12- The gem of the Taabi'een, Imaam Zuhrie عليه الرحمة narrates,

«لو جمع علم الناس كلهم و علم ازواج النبى ﷺ فكانت عائشة اوسعهم علما »

"If the knowledge of all man and the wives of Rasulullaah ﷺ were to be collected and compared to Hadhrat Aisha رضي الله عنها then Hadhrat Aisha رضي الله عنها would surpass them."

13- On another occasion he said,

«كانت عائشة اعلم الناس يسئلها الاكابر أصحاب رسول الله ﷺ»

"Hadhrat Aisha رضي الله عنها was the most knowledgeable of all people; the senior Sahabah used to refer to her."

Demise

During the Khilaafat of Hadhrat Ameer Muawiyah رضي الله عنه at the age of 68 in the month of Ramadaan 58 A.H she fell ill and passed away on 17 Ramadaan.

To Allaah do we belong and unto Him shall we return

She left a few belongings as inheritance amongst which was a portion of land which she inherited from her sister Hadhrat Asmaa رضي الله عنها. Hadhrat Muawiyah then purchased this land from her for one hundred thousand dirhams. Hadhrat Asmaa رضي الله عنها distributed this amount amongst her friends and relatives.

Hadhrat Aisha's Nikaah

Rasulullaah ﷺ was extremely saddened on the demise of Hadhrat Khadijah رضي الله عنها. The wife of Hadhrat Uthmaan bin Math'oon رضي الله عنه, Hadhrat Khoulah binte Hakeem رضي الله عنها came to Rasulullaah ﷺ and suggested, "Why do you not remarry, O Rasulullaah ﷺ?" When Rasulullaah ﷺ enquired as to whomhe should marry then she replied, "Awidow and a previously unmarried girl are both present and whomsoever you wish you may marry. When Rasulullaah ﷺ enquired as to who they were, she replied, "The widow is Saudah binte Zumu'ah رضي الله عنها and the previously unmarried girl is the daughter of Abu Bakr رضي الله عنه, Aisha رضي الله عنها." Rasulullaah ﷺ said, "It would be better if you find out more regarding Aisha." Hadhrat Khoulah رضي الله عنها approached Hadhrat Abu Bakr رضي الله عنه and informed him of the proposal of Rasulullaah ﷺ, on which Hadhrat Abu Bakr رضي الله عنه said, "Aisha is Rasulullaah's ﷺ niece(so how is it possible for them to marry?)" Hadhrat Khoulah رضي الله عنها returned to Rasulullaah ﷺ and informed him of the reply of Hadhrat Abu Bakr رضي الله عنه and Rasulullaah ﷺ replied, "Abu Bakr رضي الله عنه is my brother in Islaam and it is permissible to m rry the daughter of one's brother in Islaam."

When Hadhrat Abu Bakr رضي الله عنه was informed of this, he joyfully accepted the proposal for Hadhrat Aisha رضي الله عنها but since the son of Jubair bin Muth'im had already previously asked for her hand in marriage, they sought their permission first. Hadhrat Abu Bakr went to the home of Jubair bin Muth'im and asked, "You asked for the hand of Aisha for your son previously; what do you say now?" Jubair bin Muth'im and his household had not yet embraced Islaam at that juncture and his wife therefore said, "If this girl will come into our home then our son will also abandon the religion of his forefathers, which we are not ready to accept under any circumstances."

Hadhrat Abu Bakr then returned to his home and informed Hadhrat Khoulah, "I accept this proposal and Rasulullaah may perform the marriage whenever he wishes." Rasulullaah then later came to the home of Hadhrat Abu Bakr, **Hadhrat Abu Bakr performed the Nikaah and the Mehr (dowry) was set at four hundred Dirhams.**[1]

[1]'Bukhaari', 'Muslim', 'Nasaai'

Hadhrat Aisha's Hijrat to Madinah

After her marriage to Rasulullaah ﷺ, Hadhrat Aisha رضي الله عنها remained in the home of her parents for approximately three years; two years and three months while residing in Makkah and six or eight months after Hijrat while residing in Madinah. She migrated to Madinah in the following manner,

When the persecution and oppression of the Kuffaar and Mushrikeen of Makkah had exceeded all bounds and made life difficult andarduous for all the Muslims, Rasulullaah ﷺinstructed the Muslims to migrate to Madinah.

Hadhrat Aisha رضي الله عنها herself narrates the incident, "It was the daily practice of Rasulullaah ﷺ to visit our home every day, either in the morning or evening. One day he came to our house in the afternoon with his face concealed in a shawl, contrary to his normal habit. At that time Hadhrat Aisha رضي الله عنها and Hadhrat Asmaa رضي الله عنها were both sitting with their father, Hadhrat Abu Bakr رضي الله عنه. Rasulullaah ﷺ enquired as to whether it was safe to speak as he wished to discuss something confidential with him. **Hadhrat Abu Bakr ﷺ said, "There is no one else present here but your household."** Rasulullaah ﷺ entered and informed him of his intention to migrate to Madinah. Hadhrat Aisha رضي الله عنها and Hadhrat Asmaa رضي الله عنها prepared the provisions for the journey. Rasulullaah ﷺand Hadhrat Abu Bakr رضي الله عنهboth bid farewell to their hometown and set off towards Madinah, leaving their possessions and family behind in Makkah.

Once the conditions were adequate in Madinah, Rasulullaah ﷺ sent Hadhrat Zaid bin Haarithah ﵁ and Hadhrat Abu Raafi ﵁ to bring his family to Madinah. Similarly Hadhrat Abu Bakr ﵁ also sent someone to bring his family to Madinah.

Hadhrat Abdullaah bin Abu Bakr ﵁ brought his mother, Hadhrat Umie Rumaan ﵂, and sisters, Hadhrat Asmaa ﵂ and Hadhrat Aisha ﵂. The camel that Hadhrat Umie Rumaan and Hadhrat Aisha ﵂ were riding on was disobedient and began running wildly. It seemed as if Hadhrat Aisha ﵂ and Hadhrat Umie Rumaan ﵂ were going to fall at any moment.

The camel was running extremely fast and Hadhrat Umie Rumaan, out of fear for her daughter's life, began to cry. After a few miles the camel calmed down and she was put at ease.[1]

[1] 'Bukhaari'

Hadhrat Aisha comes into the home of Rasulullaah ﷺ

After migrating to Madinah, Hadhrat Aisha ﵂ remained with her family in the district of Banu Haarith ibn Khazraj. She stayed with her mother for six or eight months. Due to the change in climate, many of the Muhaajireen fell ill, including Hadhrat Abu Bakr ﵁ and Hadhrat Aisha ﵂. Hadhrat Aisha ﵂ illness increased to the extent that her hair also began to fall.

After regaining her health, Hadhrat Abu Bakr ﵁ came to Rasulullaah ﷺ and requested Rasulullaah ﷺ, "O Rasulullaah ﷺ! Why do you not summon your wife to move in with you?" Rasulullaah ﷺ replied that he did not have sufficient wealth with him to pay the Mehr. Hadhrat Abu Bakr ﵁ requested Rasulullaah ﷺ to accept the money from him.

Rasulullaah ﷺ borrowed the money from Hadhrat Abu Bakr ﵁ and sent it to Hadhrat Aisha ﵂. The women of the Ansaar then went to bring the bride to Rasulullaah ﷺ. Hadhrat Umie Rumaan ﵂ summoned Hadhrat Aisha ﵂ and she was taken to Rasulullaah ﷺ followed by an entourage.

Hadhrat Umie Rumaan held the hand of her daughter, platted her hair and then took her into the room where the women of the Ansaar were awaiting to take her to Rasulullaah ﷺ. **When she entered the room the women sang in a melodious voice,**

عَلَى الْخَيْرِ وَ الْبَرْكَةِ وَ عَلَى خَيْرِ طَائِرٍ

May your arrival be filled goodness and blessing

After sometime Rasulullaah ﷺ himself arrived. Hadhrat Asmaa binte Yazeed, who was the friend of Hadhrat Aisha ؓ, **narrates that at that time there was nothing in the house to offer Rasulullaah ﷺ except a glass of milk. This one glass of milk was given to Rasulullaah ﷺ, who took a sip from it and then offered it to Hadhrat Aisha ؓ who blushed out of shyness.** Hadhrat Asmaa ؓ narrates that she said to Hadhrat Aisha ؓ,"This is the offering of Rasulullaah ﷺ, do not decline it." Bashfully Hadhrat Aisha ؓ took the glass and drank a little from it. Rasulullaah ﷺ then instructed Hadhrat Aisha ؓto offer the milk to her friends. Her friends replied out of modesty, "We do not wish to drink it at this moment." Rasulullaah ﷺ replied, "Do not lie as each lie a person speaks is written against him."

In this manner from the Nikaah of Rasulullaah ﷺ to Hadhrat Aisha ؓto farewell every interaction was of simplicity, without any fret or fuss.[1]

[1]'Muslim', 'Abu Dawood', 'Ibn Maajah', 'Ahmed'

Rasulullaah ﷺ takes care not to disturb Hadhrat Aisha

Hadhrat Aisha ﷺ narrates that on one night when it was her turn with Rasulullaah ﷺ, he removed his shawl and shoes, placing them close to him, and laid down beside her.

He slept on his side and rested until he thought that I was asleep. Once he thought that I was asleep, slowly and silently he got out of bed, wore his shoes and left the room. He opened the door without making a sound and gently closed it when he left. "I also quickly rose from bed and followed Rasulullaah ﷺ", Hadhrat Aisha ﷺ said. Rasulullaah ﷺproceeded to Jannatul Baqee'a (the graveyard in Madinah), where he remained standing for a long time. **He then lifted his hands three times and then quickly began to return home.** Hadhrat Aisha narrates, "I rushed home as fast as I could and arrived before Rasulullaah ﷺ. I was lying down when Rasulullaah ﷺ entered and asked, "O Aisha! Why are you so restless?" I said that it was nothing. Rasulullaah ﷺ said, "Either you tell me or the All-Knowing will inform me." I replied, "May my parents be sacrificed for you" and I then related the entire incident."

Rasulullaah ﷺ asked, "So it was your shadow that I saw before me when I was returning?" Hadhrat Aisha ﷺ replied that it was indeed hers. **Rasulullaah ﷺ playfully hit my cheek, which caused me a little pain,** and then said, "Did you think that Allaah and His Rasul would be unjust towards you?"

Hadhrat Aisha replied, "As hard as one may try to conceal something, Allaah Ta'ala is aware of all one does." Rasulullaah replied, "Most definitely! Hadhrat Jibraeel came to me when you saw me in the graveyard. He called me softly and I replied to him even softer so that you would not hear. Hadhrat Jibraeel could not enter while you were notshrouded. Once I thought you were asleep, I did not wish to wake you fearing that you would be startled. Hadhrat Jibraeel said to me that My Rabb has instructed me to visit the deceased of Jannatul Baqee'a and supplicate on their behalf." Hadhrat Aisha enquired, "how to we supplicate for them?" Rasulullaah replied, "Recite,

اَلسَّلَامُ عَلٰى اَهْلِ الدِّيَارِ مِنَ الْمُؤْمِنِيْنَ وَ الْمُسْلِمِيْنَ وَ يَرْحَمُ اللهُ الْمُسْتَقْدِمِيْنَ
مِنَّا وَ الْمُسْتَاْخِرِيْنَ وَ اِنَّ اِنْ شَاءَ اللهُ لَلَاحِقُوْن

"Peace be upon the dwellers of the Mu'mineen and Muslimeen May Allaah's mercy descend upon the first and last amongst us. Undoubtedly, if Allaah wills, we will be united with you."[1]

[1]'Ahmed', 'Muslim', 'Tirmidhi', 'Nasaai'

A humorous incident

On one occasion Hadhrat Aisha and Rasulullaah had a small argument and Hadhrat Aisha folded her arms and turned away from Rasulullaah. During this time someone came and gave Rasulullaah a few dates as a gift, which he accepted.

Rasulullaah placed these dates before Hadhrat Aisha and said, "O Humairah! Here take these dates, take the name of Allaah and eat them." Hadhrat Aisha quickly replied, "What! Did I take my father's name and eat before?"

Rasulullaah on hearing this reply of Hadhrat Aisha was amused and smiled for a long time.[1]

[1]'Mustadrak Haakim'

Do you not love whom I love

Rasulullaah ﷺ to the best of his abilities was just and fair with regards to his wives, in all those affairs which were in his control. His wives wished for him to love them all the same as well whereas love is a matter of the heart, which is beyond the control of a man. Since Rasulullaah ﷺ loved Hadhrat Aisha ﵂ the most they desired to also be loved equally *(even though they were all treated equally)*.[1]

The blessed wives of Rasulullaah ﷺ requested Hadhrat Fatima ﵂ to approach Rasulullaah ﷺ in this regard. Hadhrat Fatima requested permission to enter the house of Rasulullaah ﷺ, at that time Rasulullaah ﷺ was resting next to Hadhrat Aisha ﵂. Rasulullaah ﷺ granted her permission to enter and she said to Rasulullaah ﷺ, "Your other wives have requested me to speak to you on their behalf to be fair with regards to the daughter of Abu Quhaafah (i.e. Hadhrat Aisha ﵂."

Rasulullaah ﷺ replied, "O beloved daughter! Do you not love whom I love?" Hadhrat Fatima ﵂ replied that she most certainly does, on which Rasulullaah ﷺ said, "Then love Aisha." When Hadhrat Fatima ﵂ heard this reply from

[1] 'Ash-Sharah lil Imaam Nawawi'

Rasulullaah ﷺ, she went to inform all the blessed wives of Rasulullaah ﷺ.

The blessed wives of Rasulullaah ﷺ again requested Hadhrat Fatima (RA) to approach Rasulullaah ﷺ and again request him to be fair (in his love). However since Hadhrat Fatima (RA) had already understood the love which Rasulullaah ﷺ had for Hadhrat Aisha (RA) from the previous encounter, she declined and said, "I take an oath by Allaah! I will never approach Rasulullaah ﷺ in this regard again."

The blessed wives of Rasulullaah ﷺ then instructed Hadhrat Zainab binte Jahash (RA) to speak to Rasulullaah ﷺ in this regard. Hadhrat Aisha narrates, "It was Zainab binte Jahash (RA) who used to compete with me for the love of Rasulullaah ﷺ, and I have never seen any women more pious, Allaah fearing, truthful and maintaining family ties than Zainab binte Jahash (RA)."

Hadhrat Zainab binte Jahash (RA) came to Rasulullaah ﷺ and requested permission to enter. Rasulullaah was still resting next to Hadhrat Aisha (RA), in the same manner as he was when Hadhrat Fatima (RA) had entered. Rasulullaah ﷺ granted her permission to enter and after entering she said to Rasulullaah ﷺ, "Your wives have sent me seeking fairness with regards to the daughter of Abu Quhaafah."[1]

[1] 'Bukhaari', 'Muslim'

Watching the Abyssinians play

Hadhrat Aisha narrates that Rasulullaah had come to her, when they heard a lot of noise and the chattering of children. When she looked to see what was happening then she saw an Abyssinian woman playing with the children and dancing with them. A few people had gathered to watch her. Rasulullaah called Hadhrat Aisha, "O Aisha! Come here and see." Hadhrat Aisha leaned on Rasulullaah, placing her cheek on the shoulder of Rasulullaah, and watched the spectacle.

After sometime Rasulullaah asked Hadhrat Aisha if she had seen enough and she replied that she wished to see more. She says, "I did not say this because I wished to see more but rather I wanted to see how much Rasulullaah loved her and how much regard he had for me."

While we were watching, Hadhrat Umar happened to pass by and dues to his awe inspiring person people began to disperse. **Rasulullaah said, "I am looking at the Shayaateen from man and Jinn fleeing out of fear for Umar ."** Thereafter Hadhrat Aisha returned to her room.[1]

[1]'Tirmidhi'

Rasulullaah ﷺ saying that he is seeing the Shayaateen of men and Jinn all fleeing means that they were all preoccupied with sport and play, which even though not Haraam is not liked. **If it were Haraam then Rasulullaah ﷺ would never have watched it or allowed Hadhrat Aisha رضي الله عنها to do the same.**[1]

[1]'Tuhfatul Ahwathi'

Hijaab from her foster uncle

Hadhrat Aisha narrates, "My foster father, Abul Qa'ees, had a brother by the name of Aflah, who came to visit me after the law of Hijaab was revealed. He sought permission to enter and I said to him that until I verify his position in light of the Shari'ah, I will not permit him to enter."

When Rasulullaah arrived, Hadhrat Aisha explained the situation to him. Rasulullaah replied, "What has prevented you permitting him to enter, he is your foster uncle. Allow him to enter." Hadhrat Aisha said, "A male did not give me milk (which means that Aflah cannot be my family as he is not related to the women who breastfed me)" Rasulullaah replied, "Permit Aflah to enter as he is your foster uncle."[1]

[1] 'Bukhaari'

Hadhrat Aisha becomes jealous

Hadhrat Urwah t reports that Hadhrat Aisha narrated, "On one occasion Rasulullaah left the house when it was my turn to be with him. I became jealous and when he returned he could tell that I was upset. He asked me, "Aisha! What has happened that you seem to overcome by jealousy?" I replied, "Why should a woman such as myself not become jealous over such a great individual such as yourself." Rasulullaah replied, "Your Shaytaan has influenced you." Hadhrat Aisha enquired, "Is there a Shaytaan with me also?" Rasulullaah replied that there was. She then asked, "Is there a Shaytaan with every person?". When Rasulullaah again replied that there was she asked, "With you as well?" Rasulullaah replied, "Yes! With me as well but my Rabb has assisted me against him. He has embraced Islaam or I have been saved from him."[1]

[1] 'Ahmed', 'Muslim'

Hadhrat Aisha's intelligence

Hadhrat Aisha ﷺ narrates that a woman asked Rasulullaah ﷺ, "How do I wash to attain purity (during Istihaadhah)?" Rasulullaah ﷺ replied that she should use a perfumed piece of cloth and then perform Wudhu. She asked, "How do I perform Wudhu with the piece of cloth?" Rasulullaah ﷺ said, "Make wudhu with it." She again asked, "How do I make Wudhu with it?" Rasulullaah ﷺ again replied, "Make wudhu with it." Still not understanding she asked once again, "How do I make Wudhu with it?" This time Rasulullaah ﷺ recited Subhanallaah and turned away from her. Hadhrat Aisha ﷺ was present with Rasulullaah ﷺ at that time and understood what Rasulullaah ﷺ had implied. She took that women aside and explained to her what Rasulullaah ﷺ meant.[1]

[1]'Nasaai', 'Bukhaari', 'Muslim'

Hadhrat Aisha's understanding of the Quraan

On one occasion someone asked Hadhrat Aisha the meaning of this verse,

"Allaah does not place on a soul a responsibility *(duty)* except what is within its capability. It *(every soul)* shall receive to its favour that *(good acts)*which it had earned and to its harm shall be what *(sins)* it had carried out." *(Surah Baqarah: 286)*

In addition to another verse,

"Whoever commits an evil act will meet *(receive)* its punishment." *(Surah Nisaa: 123)*

The purpose of the question was actually that if the implication of the above verse is indeed true then there is no hope for mercy and forgiveness.

Hadhrat Aisha replied, "When I asked Rasulullaah about the meaning of this verse he replied, "You are the first person to enquire about this verse. The word of Allaah is true but Allaah Ta'ala forgives the minor sins of a person through the various difficulties a person faces from day to day. Whenever a Mu'min becomes ill or faces some difficulty, such that even if he places something in his pocket and forgets about it and searching for it causes him worry (then too Allaah forgives his sins on account of the slight difficulty he experienced). His condition becomes like gold which is purified from filth when taken out of the fire; so too does the believer leave this world purified from all sins.[1]

[1]'Tirmidhi'

Your mother became angry

Hadhrat Safiyyah was an excellent cook and prepared the most delicious meals. Hadhrat Aisha herself narrated that she has not seen a better cook than Hadhrat Safiyyah.

On one occasion Hadhrat Safiyyah prepared a meal and sent it to Rasulullaah, when it was the turn of Hadhrat Aisha to be Rasulullaah. Hadhrat Safiyyah sent the food in with one of Hadhrat Aisha's slaves. Hadhrat Aisha was angered by this, as it was her turn, and hit the bowl from the hand of her servant and it fell and shattered into pieces. Rasulullaah began picking up the pieces and said to the servant, "Your mother has become angry." After a little while Hadhrat Aisha calmed down and felt ashamed of her actions. She asked Rasulullaah if she could compensate for her actions. Rasulullaah replied, "A similar plate and similar food will compensate for it." Hadhrat Aisha then sent a new plate to Hadhrat Safiyyah.[1]

[1] 'Bukhaari', 'Abu Dawood', 'Nasaai'

Racing with Rasulullaah ﷺ

On one expedition Hadhrat Aisha ﵂ was in the company of Rasulullaah ﷺ. On route Rasulullaah ﷺ ordered all the Sahabah to move ahead. Thereafter he said to Hadhrat Aisha ﵂, "Let us race and see who is faster." Hadhrat Aisha was thin at that time and won the race. Rasulullaah ﷺ remained silent and did not say anything to her. A few years later on another expedition, Rasulullaah ﷺ again told the Sahabah to move ahead and challenged Hadhrat Aisha ﵂ to a race. On this occasion Rasulullaah ﷺ beat her and smiling he turned to her and said, "This is for the defeat of that day."[1]

[1]'Abu Dawood', 'Ibn Maajah'

Revelation descended on her bed

Rasulullaah ﷺ loved Hadhrat Aisha dearly, which is why whenever any person wished to give a gift to Rasulullaah ﷺ then they would wait for the turn of Hadhrat Aisha. The other wives of Rasulullaah ﷺ were not pleased by this and came to Hadhrat Umie Salamah and said, "O Umie Salamah! People wait for the turn of Aisha to give gifts to Rasulullaah ﷺ. Just as Aisha enjoys this generosity so too do we desire to enjoy this generosity. Suggest to Rasulullaah that he should inform the people that they should not wait for the turn of Aisha but rather send the gift on whoever's turn it is."

Hadhrat Umie Salamah suggested this to Rasulullaah ﷺ when the opportunity presented itself and Rasulullaah ﷺ turned away from her as she said this. After some time Rasulullaah ﷺ turned towards again and she suggested the same as before and once again Rasulullaah ﷺ turned away from her. After this happened for the third time, Rasulullaah ﷺ replied, "Do not cause me pain with regards to Aisha because undoubtedly revelation does not descend upon me when I am on the bed of any of my wives except Aisha, besides her revelation does not descend when I am with any of my other wives."[1]

[1]'Bukhaari'

In other narrations it is mentioned that the blessed wives of Rasulullaah ﷺ requested Hadhrat Fatima ﵂ to speak to Rasulullaah ﷺ. When she took this message to Rasulullaah ﷺ then he said to her, "Do you not love whom I love?" this was sufficient for Hadhrat Fatima ﵂, who returned and never brought up this matter again.

Concern for the Aakhirah is purpose of life

Hadhrat Qaasim bin Muhammed bin Abu Bakr ﷺ, who is the grandson of Hadhrat Abu Bakr ﷺ, relates that it was his daily practice to greet his Aunt Hadhrat Aisha before departing for work. One day when he came to visit her as usual, he found that she was performing Chaasht Salaah and reciting the following verse,

> "However Allaah favoured us and saved us from the punishment of the scorching wind." *(Surah Toor: 27)*

She was overcome by this verse and kept reciting it repeatedly, weeping more each time. "I waited for some time for her to complete her Salaah but after much time had elapsed, "I thought to myself let me finished my work and greet her when I return."

Hadhrat Qaasim bin Muhammed رحمه الله went to the marketplace, completed his work and when he returned he found her still engaged in Salaah, reciting the same verse and still weeping.[1]

---

[1] 'Mustadrak Haakim'

Rasulullaah ﷺ passes away in the lap of Hadhrat Aisha

On one occasion Rasulullaah ﷺ came into the house and Hadhrat Aisha ﷺ was standing because she had a headache. Rasulullaah ﷺ then said, "My head is aching" and that was the beginning of Rasulullaah's ﷺ final illness and soon thereafter Rasulullaah left this worldly abode. During his final illness he kept asking which one of his wives turn it was and they soon understood that he was awaiting the turn of Hadhrat Aisha ﷺ. On account of this Rasulullaah ﷺ was moved to the room of Hadhrat Aisha ﷺ and remained there until his demise. **Rasulullaah ﷺ passed away in the room of Hadhrat Aisha ﷺ with his blessed head in the lap of Hadhrat Aisha ﷺ.**[1]

[1]'Bukhaari', 'Muslim', 'Tirmidhi'

Hadhrat Aisha defends Rasulullaah

It has been the habit of the Yahood to cause harm to Islaam and Rasulullaah ﷺ from the early days of Islaam. In accordance with their evil habit, one day a group of Yahood came to Rasulullaah ﷺ and displaying the inner filth of themselves said, "As-Saamu Alaikum" (which means death upon you). It just happened that Hadhrat Aisha ﷺ was also present there at that time and understood what was their intention by saying "As-Saamu Alaikum" and what it meant. She was furious and immediately replied to them, "May death be upon you and may you be cursed." Hearing this Rasulullaah ﷺ remarked, "There is no need for offensive language. Allaah Ta'ala loves gentleness, and I said in reply to them, "And upon you" returning there curse back to them. My supplication against them can be accepted whereas their supplication against me will never be accepted."[1]

[1]'Bukhaari', 'Muslim', 'Tirmidhi', 'Ibn Maajah'

O Rabb! I cannot say anything to him

Once Hadhrat Aisha رضي الله عنها and Hadhrat Hafsah رضي الله عنها accompanied Rasulullaah ﷺ on a journey and whenever the caravan would stop to rest, **Rasulullaah ﷺ would visit Hadhrat Aisha رضي الله عنها in her carriage and converse with her until the caravan began to travel again.**One day Hadhrat Hafsah رضي الله عنها suggested to Hadhrat Aisha رضي الله عنها that they should change carriages and she agreed. When the night set in, Rasulullaah ﷺ came to the carriage of Hadhrat Aisha رضي الله عنها as was his routine only to discover that Hadhrat Hafsah رضي الله عنها was sitting in it instead of Hadhrat Aisha رضي الله عنها. Rasulullaah ﷺ greeted her and sat down beside her.

On the other hand Hadhrat Aisha رضي الله عنهاwas awaiting the arrival of Rasulullaah ﷺ in her carriage. After sometime her patience ran out and unable to restrain herself, she stepped out of the carriage and said, "O my Rabb! I cannot say anything to him (it is no fault of Rasulullaah ﷺ as I changed my carriage), let some snake or scorpion sting me (so that Rasulullaah ﷺ will return to me)."[1]

[1] 'Bukhaari'

Hadhrat Aisha's affection and candour with the other wives of Rasulullaah ﷺ

Hadhrat Aisha ﵂ narrates that on one occasion she prepared Hareerah (a type of sweetmeat made by the Arabs) for Rasulullaah ﷺ and Hadhrat Saudah ﵂ also happened to be present in the house at that time. When she placed the sweetmeat before Rasulullaah ﷺ she invited Hadhrat Saudah ﵂also to partake of it but she refused. Hadhrat Aisha ﵂ insisted that she also partake of it and Hadhrat Saudah adamantly refused. Hadhrat Aisha then said, "If you do not eat from the sweetmeat then I will rub it on your face." However Hadhrat Saudah ﵂ stilled refused, so Hadhrat Aisha ﵂ placed her hands in the sweetmeat and rubbed it on her face." Rasulullaah ﷺ laughed as he witnessed this spectacle.

Hadhrat Saudah ﵂ narrates that Rasulullaah ﷺ then said to her, "You also rub it in the face of Aisha". She then placed her hands in the sweetmeat and rubbed it in the face of Hadhrat Aisha ﵂, on which Rasulullaah ﷺ laughed just as he laughed when Hadhrat Aisha ﵂did it. While this was occurring Hadhrat Umar happened to pass by, calling out to Abdullaah. "Thinking that Hadhrat Umar might visit Rasulullaah ﷺ instructed us to wash up."[1]

---

[1]'Abu Ya'ala', 'Ibn Asaakir', 'Kanzul Ummaal'

Rasulullaah ﷺ teases Hadhrat Aisha

On one occasion, during the final illness of Rasulullaah ﷺ, Hadhrat Aisha رضي الله عنها had a headache. Rasulullaah ﷺ said to her, "O Aisha! If you pass away before me then I will perform your Ghusal with my hands, shroud you and bury you myself and then supplicate for you. Hadhrat Aisha رضي الله عنها replied, "O Rasulullaah ﷺ! You joke at my death;if it were to occur then you will bring a new wife to come live in this home." Rasulullaah ﷺsmiled on hearing this.[1]

[1]'Bukhaari', 'Muslim'

Hadhrat Aisha is envious of Hadhrat Khadijah

Once Rasulullaah ﷺ was praisingHadhratKhadijah and continued praising her for a very long time. Hadhrat Aisha narrates that she became envious and said, "O Rasulullaah ﷺ! Why do you continue to praise an old woman from the old women of the Quraish whose lips were red and passed away a long time ago. Allaah Ta'ala has granted you better wives than her."

The face of Rasulullaah ﷺ changed on hearing this and said, "This is that wife of mine who brought Imaan in me when all others denied me. When everyone called me a liar she testified to my truthfulness. When all refused to assist me, she used all her wealth in my aid. She is the wife who granted me children whereas my other wives did not."[1]

[1]'Ahmed'

A sterling example of obedience to Rasulullaah ﷺ

In the nine years that Hadhrat Aisha ﵂ lived with Rasulullaah ﷺ she never disobeyed Rasulullaah ﷺ even once such that even if she understood something to be disliked by Rasulullaah ﷺ from his manner, she abstained from that as well.

On one occasion Hadhrat Aisha ﵂ with much enthusiasm put up a curtain containing pictures on the door of the house. When Rasulullaah ﷺ intended to visit her, his gaze fell in the curtain and immediately signs of anger and disapproval became apparent on his face.

Seeing this Hadhrat Aisha ﵂ was worried and asked, "O Rasulullaah ﷺ! Forgive my shortcomings and inform me of what I have done to displease you?" Rasulullaah ﷺ replied, "The angles do not enter the home which has pictures in it." As soon as Rasulullaah ﷺ said this she removed the curtain and cut it into pieces.

Hadhrat Aisha scolds another person

When Hadhrat Ja'far ﷺ was made Shaheed then his relatives began wailing over his death. A person came and informed Rasulullaah ﷺ, who was also saddened by his death, about their actions. Rasulullaah ﷺ instructed him to proceed and prohibited them from doing so. The person proceeded to prevent them from doing so but they still did not abstain from their wailing and mourning. He returned to Rasulullaah ﷺ and informed him that they refuse to abstain from their wailing. Rasulullaah ﷺ instructed him to prohibit them from doing so a second time but they still did not listen to him and he once again complained to Rasulullaah ﷺ. On the third occasion Rasulullaah ﷺ instructed him to throw sand in their mouths.

Hadhrat Aisha ﷺ was listening to the entire conversation and she angrily scolded the person saying, "May your nose be rubbed in the sand! You neither do what Rasulullaah has told you to do and nor do you stop annoying."[1]

The meaning of Hadhrat Aisha's ﷺ statement is that you are unable to fulfil the instruction which Rasulullaah ﷺ has given you but instead of explaining your inability of fulfilling it and requesting Rasulullaah ﷺ to send someone else in your place, you continue making the same complaint.

---

[1]'Bukhaari'

A noble mother and a noble daughter

Hadhrat Aisha ﵁ narrates that on one occasion all the blessed wives of Rasulullaah ﷺ were present when Hadhrat Fatima ﵁ arrived. Her manner of walking was exactly like that of Rasulullaah ﷺ, with not even a slight difference. Rasulullaah ﷺ greeted Hadhrat Fatima ﵁ with deep affection and asked her to sit next to him. He then whispered something in her ear, which caused her to weep and on seeing her grief, he again whispered in her ear and she smiled.

Hadhrat Aisha ﵁ narrates that she said to Hadhrat Fatima ﵁, "O Fatima! Rasulullaah ﷺ chose to confide in you from all his present here and still you weep (thus be happy and do not grieve)." After Rasulullaah ﷺ left Hadhrat Aisha ﵁ enquired from Hadhrat Fatima ﵁ what they had discussed and Hadhrat Fatima ﵁ said, "I will not divulge the secret of my father."

Later after the demise of Rasulullaah ﷺ, Hadhrat Aisha ﵁ again enquired from Hadhrat Fatima ﵁ about the secret which Rasulullaah ﷺ had confided in her saying, "O Fatima! By the right which I have over you, I ask you to inform me of what Rasulullaah ﷺ discussed with you on that day." Hadhrat Fatima ﵁ replied, "Yes, now it is possible. I wept because Rasulullaah ﷺ had informed me that his demise was close and

I smiled because he said to me, "Will you not be pleased in that you will be the leader of all women in paradise."[1]

[1]'Muslim'

Astonishing laughter

The Banu Quraizah were a Jewish tribe who had signed a treaty to assist Rasulullaah ﷺ in battle but continually failed to honour this treaty. In fact they opposed it and assisted the Kuffaar against the Muslims in the battle of Khandaq. After the battle of Khandaq, the Muslims attacked the forts of the Banu Quraizah and captured the entire tribe. Amongst the prisoners of this battle was a woman, who knew that her name was also included amongst those who were to be executed. Despite having knowledge that she was about to be killed, a few moments prior to her death, she went to visit Hadhrat Aisha ﵂, with whom she had an open and free conversation, laughing and smiling.

While they were talking, the woman's name was called out and she stood up and she proceeded to the execution area. Hadhrat Aisha ﵂ was surprised and asked her where she was going. She replied, "I have committed a crime and I proceeding towards the execution area to receive my punishment." She then left and was executed. Later Hadhrat Aisha ﵂ used to say, "To this day I am astonished at the laughter and amusement of this woman just before her death."[1]

[1]'Al-Bidaayah wan Nihaayah', 'Kashful Baarie'

The woman's name was Binaanah and she was the only woman who was executed on account of her murdering Hadhrat Khallaad bin Suwaid ﷺ by dropping a rock on him from the roof of her house.[1]

[1]'Kashful Baarie'

The incident of 'Ifq'

Hadhrat Aisha ﷺ narrates that when Rasulullaah ﷺ would depart on a journey then his blessed wives would draw lots to see who would accompany him. Whoever's name was drawn would accompany Rasulullaah ﷺ on that journey. She says, "On one expedition my name was drawn and I accompanied Rasulullaah ﷺ. This was after the order of hijaab was revealed. I used to remain in my carriage and it used to be picked up and taken down from the camel whenever we stopped and travelled. After the battle on our return journey, just before entering Madinah, we stopped to rest for the night. Rasulullaah ﷺ announced that we would be returning to Madinah shortly and the purpose of this announcement was so that people could begin preparing to travel. On hearing the announcement I left to relieve myself and when a great distance away from the caravan.

As I was returning to my carriage I placed my hand on my chest and found that my wedding necklace was missing. Thinking that it must have fallen off I retraced my steps in search of it. I took a lot of time searching for it and in the meantime the caravan began to move and thinking that I was in my carriage (on account of her being so light in weight) it was placed on my camel and everybody left."

"When I returned to where we had been encamped I found that everybody had already left. I sat down, thinking that as soon as they discover that I am not in the carriage they will return to where we were previously encamped to find me."

"As I was sitting there, I was overcome by sleep. A Sahabi of Rasulullaah ﷺ by the name of Hadhrat Safwaan bin Mu'athal ﵁ used to ride at the back of the army (so that he could follow the caravan and pick up anything that had been left behind) and arrived in the early morning. **He saw the silhouette of a person sleeping and when he came close he recognised me as he had seen me previously, before the order of Hijaab had been revealed."**

"When he saw me he said loudly, "To Allaah do we belong and unto Him shall we return", which woke me and **I covered my face with my veil.** He said nothing else to me but this and dismounted from his steed and gestured towards me to mount it. Walking ahead he pulled the animal and in this condition we travelled until we were reunited with the caravan, which had stopped for a rest."

"In essence those who were going to be destroyed on account of their perception of me were destroyed and the one who played the biggest role in false accusing me was Abdullaah bin Ubay bin Sulool."

Hadhrat Aisha ﵂ narrates, "We then arrived in Madinah after which I remained ill for a month. During this time the orchestrators of the false accusation had fabricated their tale and were spreading their falsehood everywhere. Nevertheless I still remained unaware of what was transpiring. However I had some doubt while I was ill because I did not receive the same care and affection from Rasulullaah ﷺ which I used to receive. Rasulullaah ﷺ would only come visit, greet and enquire about my well-being, after which he would turn and leave."

"This made me think that something was wrong but I was unaware of how serious it really was."

"When I felt a little better and went to relieve myself, accompanied by Hadhrat Umie Misthah, and we used to only leave to relieve ourselves in the night as in those days we did not have lavatories close to the home as it was disliked. Nevertheless I left accompanied by Umie Misthah and when we returning then Hadhrat Umie Misthah tripped over her shawl. As she fell she said, **"May Misthah be destroyed." I turned to her and said, "You have said a grave statement indeed. Do you speak ill of such a person who participated in the Battle of Badr?"** She replied, "Are you not aware of what Misthah is saying?" I enquired about what he was saying and to my horror she informed me of what he had been saying, which only worsened my health when I returned home."

"Later when Rasulullaah arrived and enquired about my health, **I asked his permission to stay at the home of my parents.** My purpose of this was to ascertain the truth of these rumours. Rasulullaah permitted me to leave and when I reached the home of my parents, I asked them about the rumours. My mother said to me, "My beloved daughter! Do not be grieved by these rumours as it rarely occurs that when a beautiful girl is with such a man who loves her and cares for her that people do not find faults in her." I replied, "Subhanallaah! Are people actually making such accusations?" I wept that entire night, neither did my tears cease nor did i sleep. My every night thereafter was spent like this, my tears not ceasing and my eyes not closing. My father tried to console me saying that my weeping will not bring me solace and my mother tried to make me sleep. My modesty made me feel like throwing myself into a well."

Even though the innocence and chastity of Hadhrat Aisha رضي الله عنها was accepted and believed, **still investigation into the matter was necessary in order to seal the mouths of the troublemakers.** It is for this reason that Rasulullaah ﷺ called Hadhrat Ali bin Abi Taalib رضي الله عنه and Hadhrat Usaamah bin Zaid رضي الله عنه seeking their console as they were of Rasulullaah's ﷺ household. Revelation had been halted during this period. They both came to Rasulullaah ﷺ and testified to the purity and chastity of Hadhrat Aisha رضي الله عنها according to their knowledge and the household of Rasulullaah ﷺ. Hadhrat Usaamah رضي الله عنه said, "Hadhrat Aisha is your wife and we know only good about her." The testimony of Hadhrat Usaamah رضي الله عنه was to console Rasulullaah ﷺ and support the innocence of Hadhrat Aisha رضي الله عنها.

Hadhrat Ali رضي الله عنه on the other hand said, "O Rasulullaah ﷺ! Allaah Ta'ala has not been rigorous in this regard and if you find that your feelings for Hadhrat Aisha رضي الله عنها have changed then there are many other women and this distaste that you are feeling can also be removed by asking the servant of Hadhrat Aisha رضي الله عنها, she will correct and give true information."

Rasulullaah ﷺ called Hadhrat Bareerah رضي الله عنها who was the servant of Hadhrat Aisha رضي الله عنها and well acquainted with her. She arrived and Rasulullaah ﷺ asked her, "Bareerah! Did you ever see anything about Aisha which cast you into doubt?" Hadhrat Bareerah رضي الله عنها replied, "I take an oath by that Allaah who sent you with the truth, I have never seen anything about her that is questionable except that she is young and leaves the dough open when she sleeps and the sheep come in and eat it." (Meaning that she is so simple that there can be no question or doubt as to her innocence and chastity).

On that day Rasulullaah ﷺ addressed the Sahabah from the mimbar, seeking their assistance against Abdullaah bin Ubay bin Sulool. He said,

"O believers! Who will assist me against that person who has caused me grief with regards to my household? I take an oath by Allaah I know only good about her and they have accused such a man regarding whom I know only goodness and virtue. He never entered my home except accompanied by me."

On hearing this address of Rasulullaah ﷺ, Hadhrat Sa'ad bin Muaadh stood up and said, "O Rasulullaah ﷺ! I will assist you in this regard. If he is from the tribe of Aus then I will sever his head from this body and if he is from our brothers of the Khazraj then we will obey whatever order you give us."

On this the chief of the Khazraj, Hadhrat Sa'ad bin Ubaadah, who was the cousin of the mother of Hadhrat Hassaan and since Hadhrat Hassaan was also involved in the accusation he understood that Hadhrat Sa'ad bin Muaadh was referring to him, stood up and said, "You are wrong! By Allaah you would never kill him nor would you be able to do so. If he was from your tribe then you would most definitely cannot have killed him."

In reply to this the cousin of Hadhrat Sa'ad bi Muaadh, Hadhrat Usaid bin Hudhair stood and said to Hadhrat Sa'ad bin Ubaadah, "You are the one who is wrong! We would most certainly kill him. You must be a Munaafiq and that is why you defend the Munaafiqs."

This statement caused a huge argument to flare up and the tribes of Aus and Khazraj were on the verge of fighting each other.

Rasulullaah ﷺ instructed them all to be silent and all went quiet and Rasulullaah ﷺ also remained silent.

Hadhrat Aisha ﷺ narrates, "I continued to cry day after day and my parents continued to check on me. I could not sleep or find rest and all I could do was weep. I was crying in my mother's lap when a woman of the Ansaar came and sought permission to enter. I granted her permission to enter and she also sat by me and began to weep. It was during this time that Rasulullaah ﷺ arrived at our home and came in to see me. From the day I was falsely accused Rasulullaah ﷺ had not sat next to me and for an entire month no revelation came to Rasulullaah ﷺ. Rasulullaah ﷺ entered, recited the Shahaadah and said, "I have been informed with regards to you that if you are indeed innocent then Allaah Ta'ala will definitely testify to your innocence and if you committed any sin then repent and seek forgiveness from Allaah because when a person confesses to his sins and repents then Allaah Ta'ala most certainly forgives him."

When Rasulullaah ﷺ finished his statement my tears dried such that I did not feel like shedding a single tear. I asked my father to answer Rasulullaah ﷺ but my father said he does not know what to say to Rasulullaah ﷺ. I then asked my mother to reply on my behalf but she also excused herself until I was forced to reply for myself. I was still young at that time and had not yet learnt much of the Quraan. I said, "By Allaah I know very well that you all have been listening to these rumours until it has entered into your hearts and you also believe it to an extent. Now if I tell you that I am innocent you all will not believe me and if I confess to that of which I am Innocent then you all will say she has spoken the truth. I find no example of our situation except what has been mentioned regarding the matter of Hadhrat Yusuf عليه السلام when Hadhrat Yaqoob عليه السلام heard the false testimony of his sons and replied, "I will wait patiently and I seek Allaah's assistance from all that you describe"."

After saying this Hadhrat Aisha ﵂ left the room and rested in her bed. She says, "I had full conviction that Allaah Ta'ala was aware of my innocence and Allaah will testify to it but I never imagined that Allaah Ta'ala will reveal Quraan in this regard as I thought myself beneath such an honour that Allaah Ta'ala Himself will speak on my behalf. Undoubtedly I had hoped that Rasulullaah ﷺ would be shown a dream, through which my innocence will be proven but I take an oath by Allaah, Rasulullaah ﷺ had not even moved when revelation began to descend on him. He was gripped by the intensity of revelation as it always would grip him such that perspiration like pearls began to stream from his blessed forehead, despite the day being cold." This was on account of the immense weight of the revelation of the Quraan.

Hadhrat Aisha ﵂ narrates that once revelation was complete, Rasulullaah smiled and the first thing he said was, "Aisha Allaah Ta'ala has revealed your innocence." My mother instructed me to stand in respect of Rasulullaah ﷺ but I replied that I will not stand except for Allaah, to praise and glorify Him as Allaah Ta'ala revealed my innocence." Allaah Ta'ala said,

"It was indeed a *(hypocritical)* group from you that brought *(initiated)* the slander *(the accusation against Hadhrat Aisha ﵂)*."

When Allaah Ta'ala revealed these verse of her innocence then Hadhrat Abu Bakr ﵁, who assisted Hadhrat Misthah ﵁ financially , said, "I take an oath by Allaah I will never assist Misthah ever again as he also falsely accused Aisha." On this the verse was revealed,

"The high ranking and wealthy ones' among you *(like Abu Bakr* ﷺ*)* should not take an oath not to spend on their relatives, the poor and those who migrate in Allah's path. They should *(rather)* forgive and pardon. Do you not like to forgive you? Allaah is Most forgiving, Most Merciful."

Hadhrat Abu Bakr ﷺ said, "I would most certainly love to be forgiven, it is my desire that Allaah forgive me." It is mentioned that Hadhrat Abu Bakr ﷺ then continued to spend on Hadhrat Misthah ﷺ and never stopped spending on him.

Hadhrat Aisha ﷺ narrates that Rasulullaah ﷺ also enquired about her from Hadhrat Zainab binte Jahash ﷺ and she replied, "I shut my ears and eyes from such talks. I know only good about her."

Hadhrat Aisha ﷺ narrates that from all the blessed wives of Rasulullaah ﷺ, it was Hadhrat Zainab ﷺ who used to compete with her for the affection of Rasulullaah ﷺ but Allaah Ta'ala saved her (from being ensnared in this mischief) on account of her Taqwa and piety."[1]

The following verse was revealed in honour of Hadhrat Aisha ﷺ,

"(Referring to the accusation of adultery that some Munafiqeen directed at Hadhrat Aisha ﷺ, the wife of Rasulullaah ﷺ Allaah says,) It was indeed a (hypocritical) group from you that brought (initiated) the slander (the accusation against Hadhrat Aisha ﷺ). Do not regard it (the accusation) as a misfortune, for it was good for you (although the slander caused grief to the Muslims and particularly to Aisha ﷺ, it was good for them because they earned tremendous rewards by exercising

[1]'Bukhaari'

patience and having a lesson taught to the entire Ummat). Every one of them (those who actively accused her) will have his share of(punishment for) the sin (of slander) which he earned. (However) A terrible punishment shall be for the one who took the greatest part in it (who was the leader of the Munafiqeen, Abdullah bin Ubay bin Sulool).

(Instead of listening to the accusation, thereby giving courage to the slanderers) Why did the Mu'mineen men and women not think favourably of themselves (of those who were accused) when they heard about it, and say (about the accusation), "This is clear defamation!"?

Why have they *(the accusers)* not presented four witnesses *(to testify that they had witnessed the act of adultery)*? Since they have not presented four witnesses then these people are surely liars in Allaah's sight*(because they had not proven anything according to Shari'ah)*.

If it were not for Allaah's grace upon you *(Muslims by granting you the ability to repent)*, and for His mercy in this world and in the Aakhirah, a dreadful punishment *(disaster)* would have afflicted you because of what *(slander)* you involved yourselves in."

If you seek my company in Jannat

One day a person gave Rasulullaah afew dates as a gift, which have been mentioned in Hadeeth to have numbered 9 or 11. Hadhrat Aisha and Rasulullaah had not eaten for a number of days but despite her intense hunger Hadhrat Aisha did not eat the date and kept them for Rasulullaah. When Rasulullaah returned home then Hadhrat Aisha presented the dates to him. Rasulullaah ate the dates but later enquired, "Aisha! Did you eat anything?" Hadhrat Aisha replied, "O Rasulullaah! The pleasure of my Rabb is sufficient for me." Rasulullaah understood that this meant she had not eaten anything and was saddened by this. He said to her, "You should have also eaten from the dates." Hadhrat Aisha smiled and asked lovingly, "Has Rasulullaah eaten?" Rasulullaah was moved by her affection and supplicated to Allaah, "O Allaah! Reward Aisha abundantly for her patience." Hadhrat Aisha asked O Rasulullaah! Ask Allaah Ta'ala to make me your wife in Jannat as well." Rasulullaah replied, "If you seek my company in Jannat then be patient and abstinent. Do not collect provisions for tomorrow and spend in Allah's path whatever exceeds your needs.

After hearing this advice of Rasulullaah ﷺ, Hadhrat Aisha رضي الله عنها practised upon it throughout her life with her heart and soul.[1]

[1]'Mustadrak Haakim'

Preference to her brothers and sisters

Hadhrat Aisha رضي الله عنها narrates that Hadhrat Abu Bakr رضي الله عنه had separated a portion of the dates from the date of his garden in Ghaabah to be given to her as a gift but when Hadhrat Abu Bakr's رضي الله عنه time of death drew nearer he called for her and said, "O my beloved daughter! I love none more than you and the difficulty of none worries me after my death but yours. I had separated a portion of dates to be given away to you as a gift. If you take those dates today and keep it for yourself then it is yours but if you leave it then it is inheritance and has to be share between your two sisters and two brothers in accordance with the laws of the Quraan."

Hadhrat Aisha رضي الله عنها replied, "My beloved father! Even if you were to have given me more than that as a gift, I still would not have touched it so that it could be distributed as inheritance. However I have only one sister, Asmaa, who is the other sister?" Hadhrat Abu Bakr رضي الله عنه replied, "Your other sister is the sister my wife, Habeebah binte Khaarijah رضي الله عنها is carrying." Gesturing towards her, Hadhrat Abu Bakr رضي الله عنه said, "I think that it will be a girl." Later is occurred exactly as he thought and Hadhrat Umie Kulthoom binte Abu Bakr was born.[1]

---

[1] 'Baihaqi', 'Muwatta Imaam Maalik'

Hundred thousand dirhams in a day

On one occasion someone gave Hadhrat Aisha ﷺ one hundred thousand dirhams as a gift. Hadhrat Aisha ﷺ asked for a tray and filled it with dirhams and began distributing it and continued to do so until there was not a single Dirham left that night.

Hadhrat Aisha ﷺ happened to be fasting that day and instructed her slave to bring her something to terminate her fast with at the end of the day. The slave brought one piece of bread and olive oil and said to Hadhrat Aisha ﷺ, "How nice it could have been if we just kept one dirham and used it to purchase a little meat for today." Hadhrat Aisha ﷺ replied, "What benefit is it by speaking now, had you spoken earlier then I would have sent you to purchase it."[1]

[1]'Hikaayat Sahabah'

Eat from this, it is better than your bread

One day Hadhrat Aisha ﷺ was fasting when a poor person came to her asking for food. At that time there was only one piece of bread in the house. Hadhrat Aisha ﷺ ordered her slave to give the bread to the poor person. The slave replied that there will be nothing left for her to break her fast as there only remained this one piece of bread.

Hadhrat Aisha ﷺ replied, "Never mind, still give the bread to the poor person." The slave narrates that she gave the bread away and later that day such a person, who would not ordinarily give Sadaqah, came and gave them an entire cooked sheep with plenty bread. Hadhrat Aisha ﷺ called the slave and said, "Eat from this, it is better than your bread."[1]

[1] 'Muwatta Imaam Maalik'

The reply from above

Hadhrat Aisha ﷺ narrates, "Great indeed is that Being who hears everything. I was listening to Hadhrat Khoulah binte Tha'labah but sometimes I could hear and other times I could not. She was complaining to Rasulullaah ﷺ about her husband saying, "O Rasulullaah ﷺ! My husband has used up all my wealth, finished my youth, and I have borne him many children but now when I have gone old and can no longer bear children, he has made Thihaar[1] with me. O Allaah I complain to you about him."

Hadhrat Aisha ﷺ narrates, "Hadhrat Khoulah had not yet moved from there when Hadhrat Jibraeel ﷺ descended with revelation,

"Allaah had certainly heard the speech of the lady who debated with you *(O Rasulullaah ﷺ)* concerning her husband and who complained to Allaah. Allah was listening to your discussion. Verily Allaah is All Hearing, All Seeing"[2]

In another narration it is mentioned that when Hadhrat Khoulah ﷺ came to Rasulullaah ﷺ, Hadhrat Aisha ﷺ was washing the

[1]When one compares his wife to a blood relative, which was considered a divorce before the laws regarding it were revealed.
[2]'Bukhaari', 'Tafseer Ibn Katheer'

right side of his head. When Hadhrat Khoulah complained to Allaah of her plight then Hadhrat Aisha began washing the left side of Rasulullaah's head, saying to Hadhrat Khoulah, "Stop talking and stop complaining, do you not see the face of Rasulullaah?" Soon after that revelation completed and Rasulullaah called her husband and explained the laws of Thihaar to him.[1]

[1]'Tafseer l-Khaazin'

None will be remembered in three places

Hadhrat Aisha says that she was once thinking of Jahannam and began weeping. Rasulullaah enquired, "O Aisha! What makes you weep?" I replied, "I am weeping out of fear for Jahannam. Will you remember your family on the Day of Qiyaamah?"

Rasulullaah replied, "There are three places where no person will remember anyone;

"When one's deeds will be weighed until it is established that his deeds are heavy or light."

"When a person receives his book of deeds he will not remember anybody until it is ascertained whether he will receive it in his left hand or right hand. Those who receive it in their rights hands will say "Here read it!"

"When crossing the Pul-Siraat nobody will remember any other until it is established that he has been saved or not. When the Pul-Siraat is placed over Jahannam and on both sides will be hooks and thorns. Whoever Allaah wishes will become ensnared in those hooks and thorns and prevented from moving forward."[1]

---

[1]'Mustadrak Haakim'

Praise for the Ansaar women

Hadhrat Safiyyah binte Shaibah narrates that she was sitting with Hadhrat Aisha ؓ talking about the women of the Quraish; enumerating their virtues. Hadhrat Aisha ؓ said, "Undoubtedly the women of the Quraish have great merit but I have never seen anyone surpass the women of the Ansaar in testifying to the Quraan and brining Imaan in it." When the following verse of Surah Noor was revealed,

"And they should wear their scarves over their bosoms *(to cover their heads as well as their chests, unlike the scarves worn during the period of Ignorance, which only covered the head)*."

The men of the Ansaar went home and informed their wives of the order of Allaah revealed in this verse. Each one of them recited this verse to their wives, sisters, daughters and women of the house, and they all testified to it and brought Imaan in it as soon as they heard it. They immediately practised upon it and taking sheets they concealed themselves entirely in it.

The following morning for Fajr Salaah, they all stood behind Rasulullaah ﷺ wrapped in their sheets as if they had crows sitting on their heads."[1]

---

[1] 'Abu Dawood', 'Ibn Abi Haatim', 'Tafseer Ibn Katheer'

Hadhrat Aisha listens to recitation of the Quraan

Hadhrat Aisha narrates that on one night she took a little longer in returning to Rasulullaah ﷺ and when she returned Rasulullaah ﷺ enquired as to where she had been. She replied, "One of your Sahabah was reciting the Quraan in the Masjid and I was listening to his recitation (because of which I was late). I have never heard such a melodious voice and such beautiful recitation from any of your other Sahabah."

Rasulullaah ﷺ stood and accompanied Hadhrat Aisha to the Masjid and they both listened to the recitation of the Sahabi for a long time. Rasulullaah ﷺ then turned to Hadhrat Aisha and said, "This is Saalim, the slave of Abu Hudhaifah, all praise belongs to Allaah who has created such a person from amongst my Ummat."[1]

[1]'Mustadrak Haakim', 'Hayaatus Sahabah'

Hadhrat Aisha in the field of jihaad

The virtues and excellent qualities of Hadhrat Aisha ﵂ fill the pages of history. She was a master in the field of fiqh and in deriving the rulings of Shari'ah. An intelligent woman, capable and apt, possessing the character of Rasulullaah ﷺ. Her life story also tells great tales of daring exploits in the field of Jihaad.

During the Battle of Uhud in 3 A.H, when the tides of the battle turned against the Muslims and news spread that Rasulullaah ﷺ had been martyred, Hadhrat Aisha ﵂ and a few other women, after hearing the news in Madinah, rushed into the battle field with no concern or fear for their lives. After reaching the battlefield and finding Rasulullaah ﷺ, she tended to his wounds and gave Rasulullaah ﷺ and others who were injured water to drink.

Hadhrat Anas ﵁ narrates that he saw Hadhrat Aisha ﵂ and Hadhrat Umie Sulaim ﵂ running to and from during the battle of Uhud, their trousers were slightly raised and he could see their anklets around their ankles.

After some time the Sahabah regrouped and surrounded Rasulullaah ﷺ, and Hadhrat Aisha as well as the other women then returned to Madinah.[1]

---

[1]'Taareekh Thabri', 'Hayaatus Sahabah'

The mesmerizing effect of gazing at Rasulullaah ﷺ

Hadhrat Aisha رضي الله عنها says that Rasulullaah ﷺ was once repairing his shoes and she was using the spinning wheel, when her gaze happened to fall on Rasulullaah's ﷺ blessed face. She saw a few drops of perspiration on the face of Rasulullaah ﷺ and each drop had a light radiating from it. Hadhrat Aisha رضي الله عنها narrates, "This was such a beautiful scene for me that I was left mesmerized, gazing at the blessed face of Rasulullaah ﷺ. Rasulullaah ﷺ then lifted his gaze and saw that I was staring at him. He asked, "O Aisha! What is the matter? Why do you stare at me looking so amazed?" I replied, "O Rasulullaah ﷺ! I was staring at your face, looking at the drops of perspiration on your forehead which seems to be radiating with Noor (divine light). This beautiful scene has transfixed my gaze upon you. I take an oath by Allaah; if Abu Kabeer Hadhali (a poet from the period of ignorance) were to have seen you then he would have understood that the true personification of his poetry was you."

Rasulullaah ﷺ asked Hadhrat Aisha رضي الله عنها to recite his poem for him and she read,

و مبئر من كل غير حيضة وفساد مرضعة و ذاء مغيل

واذا نظرت الى اسرة وجهه برقت كبرق العارض المتهلل

He is pure from the contaminations of birth and
fosterage and

When I gaze at his luminous face it seems as if
lightning and radiance is emanating from him

When Rasulullaah ﷺ heard this poem, he put down all that he was holding in his hands and said to Hadhrat Aisha ﷺ, "The pleasure and delight that your words have brought me is even greater than the joy and satisfaction you felt when gazing at me."[1]

[1]'Mustadrak Haakim', 'Madaarijus Saalikeen'

The Keeper of Rasulullaah`s ﷺ secrets

On one occasion Rasulullaah ﷺ intended to wage Jihaad against the Quraish and told Hadhrat Aisha ﷺ to make preparations for him to depart in Jihaad but to keep his preparations a secret and not divulge it to anyone. Rasulullaah ﷺ then also busied himself with preparations for Jihaad.

After a little while Hadhrat Abu Bakr ﷺ came to visit Hadhrat Aisha ﷺand she was grinding wheat. Hadhrat Abu Bakr ﷺ enquired from her the reason for doing so asking, "Is Rasulullaah ﷺ departing on a journey?" Hadhrat Aisha ﷺ remained silent and Hadhrat Abu Bakr ﷺ again asked, "Is Rasulullaah ﷺ preparing for Jihaad?" Hadhrat Aisha ﷺ still remained silent. Hadhrat Abu Bakr ﷺ then asked, "Perhaps he is intending to attack the people of Najd?" Hadhrat Aisha still remained silent and never uttered a word. Hadhrat Abu Bakr ﷺ asked, "Perhaps he is intending to attack the Quraish?" **However Hadhrat Aisha ﷺ remained silent and did not divulge the secret of Rasulullaah ﷺ to her own father also.**

During this time Rasulullaah ﷺ entered the room and Hadhrat Abu Bakr ﷺ asked him, "O Rasulullaah ﷺ! Are you intending to travel somewhere?" Rasulullaah ﷺ replied that he was, on which Hadhrat Abu Bakr ﷺ enquired, "Are you travelling towards the Romans?" Rasulullaah ﷺ said no, "Are you travelling towards the people of Najd?" asked Hadhrat Abu Bakr. Rasulullaah once again said no, on which Hadhrat Abu Bakr understood that Rasulullaah was intending to attack the Quraish.[1]

[1]'Taareekh Ibn Katheer'

The law of Tayammum revealed

Hadhrat Aisha accompanied Rasulullaah on one expedition and during the journey Hadhrat Aisha lost her necklace, the very same necklace which was lost during the incident of 'Ifq'. When the caravan was returning to Madinah and had reached Dhaatul Jaish, the necklace broke and was lost.

Hadhrat Aisha had learnt her lesson from the previous incident and this time immediately informed Rasulullaah that it has been lost (instead of going to search for it herself).It was nearly morning and Rasulullaah ordered the caravan to stop and instructed a few Sahabah to search for the necklace.

It just so happened that the area where the caravan had stopped did not contain water for many miles. As the time of Salaah drew nearer people began to get apprehensive and approached Hadhrat Abu Bakr and informed him of the situation (that there was no water and the time of Salaah was very close). Hadhrat Abu Bakr went to discuss the matter with Rasulullaah and found that he was taking rest on the lap of Hadhrat Aisha. Hadhrat Abu Bakr addresses his daughter saying, "You always get into some sort of problem" and as he said this he poked her a few times with his finger. Hadhrat Aisha did not want to disturb Rasulullaah and did not budge despite the pain she had felt. Later when Rasulullaah ﷺ awoke he as informed of what had transpired. During this time revelation began to descend upon Rasulullaah ﷺ. Before this Wudhu was the only means of attaining purification for Salaah but when Hadhrat Aisha's رضي الله عنها necklace went missing and the caravan stopped to search for it, with no water in sight for miles, the order was revealed that if water is not available to perform Wudhu then purity can be attained through Tayammum.

"If you are ill *(and unable to use water)*, on a journey, returning from the toilet or from touching *(cohabiting)* with your wives, and you do not find any water, then perform Tayammum with clean soil, passing your hands over your faces and arms. Verily Allaah is Most Pardoning , Most Forgiving." (Surah Nisaa: 43)

A few moments previously the Sahabah were worried and there was no water available, now the condition was reversed and all the Sahabah were overjoyed. They all began supplicating for the 'Mother of the believers', Hadhrat Aisha رضي الله عنها. **Later when the caravan began to move the necklace was found beneath the camel Hadhrat Aisha رضي الله عنها was riding upon.**[1]

Hadhrat Usaid bin Hudhair رضي الله عنه said to Hadhrat Aisha رضي الله عنها, "May Allaah reward you abundantly. I take an oath by Allaah! Whenever any incident occurred with you, Allaah Ta'ala created a solution for it, which was a means of blessing for all Muslims."[2]

[1]'Bukhaari'
[2]ibid

Hadhrat Aisha yearning to learn a supplication

Hadhrat Aisha رضي الله عنها narrates that Rasulullaah ﷺ said to her one day, "O Aisha! Do you know that Allaah Ta'ala has taught me one of His names that if one were to supplicate to Him using it then his supplications would most certainly be accepted?"

Hadhrat Aisha رضي الله عنها enquired, "O Rasulullaah ﷺ! May my parents be sacrificed for you. Please teach me the supplication."

Rasulullaah ﷺ replied, "O Aisha! This supplication is not appropriate for you." Hadhrat Aisha relates that she was troubled by this and sat in the corner pondering over it. She then came to Rasulullaah ﷺ and again asked to be taught the supplication. Rasulullaah ﷺ replied, "I do not think this supplication is appropriate for you, that I teach it to you and you use it to ask for worldly needs."

Hadhrat Aisha رضي الله عنها narrates that she then stood, made Wudhu and performed two Raqaats of Salaah, supplicating in the following manner,

"اللّٰهُمَّ إِنِّيْ أَدْعُوْكَ اللهَ وَ أَدْعُوْكَ الرَّحْمٰنَ وَ أَدْعُوْكَ الْبَرَّ الرَّحِيْمَ وَ أَدْعُوْكَ
بِأَسْمَائِكَ الْحُسْنٰى كُلِّهَا مَا عَلِمْتُ مِنْهَا وَ مَا لَمْ أَعْلَمْ أَنْ تَغْفِرَلِيْ وَ تَرْحَمَنِيْ"

"O Allaah! I call upon You by your name Allaah, I call upon You by you name Most Gracious, I call You by your name Most Righteous, Most Merciful. I call upon by all your beautiful names; those that I know of and those that I am unaware of that,You forgive me and have mercy upon me."

Hadhrat Aisha narrates that Rasulullaah smiled when he heard my supplication and said, "O Aisha! The blessed name is one of the names with which you just supplicated."[1]

[1]'Hayaatus Sahabah'

Hadhrat Aisha's knowledge of medicine

Hadhrat Urwah, who is the nephew of Hadhrat Aisha narrates that he asked Hadhrat Aisha, "The more I think about you the more astonished I become. When I find that you are the most knowledgeable of all people with regards to matters of Deen, I am not astonished because you are the wife of Rasulullaah and the daughter of Hadhrat Abu Bakr (and therefore you should have the most knowledge about Deen). When I learn of your knowledge of Arab history, their ancestry, and of their poetry then too I am not astonished as your father (Hadhrat Abu Bakr) was most knowledgeable of the Quraish with regards to these matters (and therefore it is no surprise that his daughter is also most knowledgeable is this regard). However what truly astonishes me is that you possess knowledge of medicine as well. From whom did you learn this?"

Hadhrat Urwah narrates that Hadhrat Aisha held his hand lovingly and addressing him affectionately said, "O Urayyah! When Rasulullaah's illness increased then doctors from amongst the Arabs and Non-Arabs began sending medication for him and in this manner I learnt about medicine."

It is reported in 'Musnad Ahmed' that in treating Rasulullaah ﷺ with their prescribed medication, she gained experience in the field of medicine.[1]

[1]'Musnad Ahmed', 'Awsaathul Kabeer'

I make this supplication for my Ummat in every Salaah

Hadhrat Aisha narrates that one day she saw Rasulullaah extremely happy and she asked him to supplicate for her. Rasulullaah supplicated in the following manner,

"O Allaah! Forgive al the sins of Aisha, past, present and future, those she committed in secret and those she committed in open."

Hadhrat Aisha narrates that she was so pleased by this supplication that she began to skip as she walked. Rasulullaah asked, "Are you so pleased with my supplication?" Hadhrat Aisha replied, "Why should I not be overjoyed with this supplication?" Pleased with the reply of Hadhrat Aisha, **Rasulullaah said, "I take an oath by Allaah! I make this supplication for my Ummat in every Salaah."**[1]

[1]'Hayaatus Sahabah'

The story of eleven women

Hadhrat Aisha once related an incident to Rasulullaah of eleven women. She said, "Once there were eleven women who promised not to conceal anything regarding their husbands and will disclose everything."

The names of these eleven women are not mentioned in any of the authentic narrations and even though their names have been mentioned a few weaker narrations, there are many discrepancies. It is for this reason that the names have been omitted in the story. It is mentioned that these women were either from Yemen or Hijaaz and their husbands had all left for to attend to some errands so they gathered together and discussed their husbands. Each woman described her husband's habits.

The first woman

The first women said, "My husband is like a useless piece of meat from a lean camel, which has been placed on a mountain top. Neither is the path to it easy that one is tempted to climb it nor is the meat of such a standard that one will brave such a journey to get to it"

Meaning that her husband is a hopeless individual, having no praiseworthy traits. Even if he is capable of something then too it is difficult to get him to do it and if he does it then too it is done haphazardly.

The second woman

"I cannot talk about my husband because I fear once I start discussing his faults I will never be able to stop; once I start I will mention his inner and outer faults."

She claimed that her husband had countless faults and then excused herself from elaborating.

The third woman

"My husband is difficult (foolish and irrational); if I say anything tohim then he divorces me and when I remain silent then he abandons me."

Meaning that whenever she asks for her needs then his temper takes control of him and he divorces her and if she remains silent and does not ask for anything then he shows no concern for her. She cannot call herself a wife nor can she call herself single and search for another husband.

The fourth woman

"My husband is like the night of Tihaamah (i.e. his is calm), neither impulsive nor over cautious. He neither fears anything nor does he shy away from anything."

This woman praised her husband saying that he is a composed individual who does not pry too much nor does he abstain completely.

The fifth woman

"My husband is like a cheetah at home and like a lion outside, and he never questions me about what he leaves in the home to use."

This woman also praised her husband that he does not interfere in her affairs in the home and does not question her about the usage of the household items.

The sixth woman

"When my husband eats he consumes everything and when he drinks he finishes everything. When he sleeps then he wraps himself in the blanket and does not even extend his hand towards me to ease my pain.'

This woman spoke ill of her husband that he serves no other purpose but eating and drinking, and even shows no concern for his wife.

The seventh woman

"My husband is incapable of intimacy. Understand this much that every illness is found in him. He is also so oppressive that he will crack my skull or would my body or even do both."

This woman also spoke ill of her husband that he is incapable of fulfilling the duties of marriage. When he speaks he curses, when you joke with him he becomes abusive and when he is angry then he even breaks her limbs.

The eighth woman

"My husband smells beautiful like saffron and when he touches me is gentle like a rabbit"

This woman praised her husband, that he is excellent in his inner and outward manner. He is passive and never gets angry, lean and gentle and fragrant.

The ninth woman

"My husband is an owner of tall houses, long in stature, and has lots of ash. His house is close to council chambers."

This woman praised her husband saying that he is a generous and esteemed personality, whose kitchen is always busy entertaining guests, which is why there is so much ash. He has a medium build, not too short or too tall. He is a person of perception and insight which is why his council is sought often as if his house is the council chambers.

The tenth woman

"My husband's name is Maalik. How excellent is Maalik? All praise will fall short of describing him. There are plenty stables for all his camels but they rarely ever have time to graze. Whenever the camels hear the sound of the bell then they know that there death is near."

The gist of this woman's statement is that her husband is extremely generous. Since he is always entertaining guests, his camels never have time to graze and remain in the stables where they are slaughtered on a daily basis, and presented before the guests.

The eleventh woman

"My husband's name is Abu Zar'a and how excellent is Abu Zar'a! He has made neck lean over with all the jewels he has made me wear and fattened my body. He has made me extremely happy that I filled with joy and happiness."

"He found me living amongst the shepherds, who lived a life of hardship on the edge of the mountains and made me the owner of horses, camels, farms, and crops. When I talk to him then he is not rude to me, when I sleep then he does not disturb me and when I drink he lets me drink to my fill."

"The mother of Abu Zur'a! How excellent is the mother of Abu Zur'a! Her containers always remain full and her home is extremely huge."

"The son of Abu Zur'a! How excellent is the son of Abu Zur'a! His bedroom is narrow like a sword and the leg of a small sheep satisfies him."

Meaning that he is brave and courageous and leads the life of a soldier, sleeping little and satisfied with a little food.

"The daughter of Abu Zar'a! How excellent is the daughter of Abu Zar'a! She is obedient to her father and dutiful to her mother. She fills her clothes (i.e. she is stout) and is the beloved of her husband, which is why she makes his other wives so jealous."

"The slave of Abu Zar'a! How excellent is the slave of Abu Zar'a! She never divulges the secrets of our home, she never takes anything without permission and she keeps us clean from dust."

"This was my condition, leading a happy life until Abu Zar'a left the home one day to fetch milk when he saw another woman on the road, with two sons like cheetahs rolling two pomegranates beneath her. In this manner Abu Zar'a was inclined to her such that he divorced me and married her."

"After Abu Zar'a divorced me, I married an honourable chief, who is the rider of magnificent horses and a brandisher of spears. He has given me many bounties and presented me with pairs of camels, cows, sheep, etc. He has also said to me, "O Umie Zar'a! Eat and send for your family to eat as well."

"However if I were to take all the gifts he has given to me then it will not even fill the smallest container of Abu Zar'a."

When Hadhrat Aisha completed relating the tale of the eleventh woman, Rasulullaah said, "I am (good) to you like how Abu Zar'a was (good) to Umie Zar'a except that I will not divorce you."

Hadhrat Aisha replied, "O Rasulullaah! May my parents be sacrificed for you! What is Abu Zar'a? You are by far greater in my eyes than Abu Zar'a."

This is also a way of showing love

On one occasion an Iranian neighbour of Rasulullaah ﷺ invited him to partake of meals at his home. Rasulullaah ﷺ replied that he would accept the invitation on condition that Hadhrat Aisha رضي الله عنها could also accompany him. The Iranian declined and Rasulullaah ﷺ said, "In that case I cannot accept your invitation."

The reason for Rasulullaah ﷺ declining the invitation was that at that time Rasulullaah's ﷺ household was in poverty and were suffering from the pangs of hunger. This is why Rasulullaah ﷺ did not think it appropriate to indulge himself in a meal and while his beloved wife was suffering from hunger at home.

The Iranian returned and again invited Rasulullaah ﷺ to join him for meals. Rasulullaah ﷺ again requested permission for Hadhrat Aisha رضي الله عنها to accompany him and when the Iranian declined, Rasulullaah also declined the invitation.

The host returned for the third time and again invited Rasulullaah ﷺ to join him for meals and when Rasulullaah ﷺ requested permission for Hadhrat Aisha رضي الله عنها to join him, this time the host granted him permission. Rasulullaah ﷺ then joined him for meals accompanied by Hadhrat Aisha رضي الله عنها.

The neighbour declined the first two times because meals had been prepared for one person only and on the third, preparations had been made to accommodate Hadhrat Aisha ﷺ as well.[1]

[1]'Muslim'

Concern for the Aakhirah

Hadhrat Sa'eed bin Musayab narrates that on one occasion Hadhrat Aisha said to Rasulullaah, "O Rasulullaah! Ever since you informed me of the fierce sound of the voices of Munkar and Nakeer as well as the condition of the grave, I have been unable to find rest. Fear of the grave and the thought of its ferocity remains with me all the time."

Hearing this Rasulullaah replied, "Aisha! The sound of the voice of Munkar and Nakeer will be pleasing to the believer just as applying Surma is pleasing to a person and the grave will be a means of comfort and solace for the believer just as a mother whose child has complained to her of pain and she holds him close to comfort him. Aisha! Destruction will only be for those who doubt the decree of Allaah. Do you know how they will be crushed in the grave?" Rasulullaah then himself said, "He will be crushed as if a huge boulder is pressing down on him."[1]

[1]'Mishkaat'

A principle of life

Hadhrat Aisha was endowed with the qualities of wisdom and perception by Allaah Ta'ala. She practised on every instruction of Rasulullaah, an example of which is the saying of Rasulullaah, "Treat people according to their status."

Hadhrat Aisha always acted upon this. On one occasion a beggar came to Hadhrat Aisha asking for something to eat. Hadhrat Aisha gave him a piece of bread and he went on his way. After sometime another person, neatly dressed and well kept, came to her door asking for something to eat. Seeming like a person of respect, honouring his status, Hadhrat Aisha sat him down, had meals served to him and after eating he left.

Later she was asked the reason for treating each of them differently. Hadhrat Aisha replied, "Rasulullaah Has said, "Treat people according to their status."[1]

[1]'Abu Dawood'

How tiny it seems

Hadhrat Imaam Maalik ﵀ relates, "It has reached me that once a poor person asked Hadhrat Aisha ﵂ for something to eat and at that time a few grapes were in front of Hadhrat Aisha ﵂. She ordered that one of the grapes should be given to the person. The poor person was astonished when he received the one grape and just stared at it. Hadhrat Aisha ﵂ said to him, "Are you astonished at this one grape, wondering how you will be satisfied with it?" Hadhrat Aisha ﵂ the recited the verse,

"Whoever *(sincerely)* does an atoms weight of good will see it"

If one ponders over this then he will understand that deep wisdom as hidden in this statement. If a person will ponder over every single one of his actions to see how small, inferior and tiny it seems and one will be rewarded in accordance with one's actions, good actions with reward and bad actions with punishment, then this outlook can be a means of success for him in this world and Aakhirah.

Are you better looking or your two wives

Before the order of Hijaab was revealed a young man, who was physically unattractive and a little unsightly, came to Rasulullaah ﷺ. He pledged his allegiance to Rasulullaah ﷺ. At that time Rasulullaah ﷺ was in the home of Hadhrat Aisha ﷺ and she was sitting alongside him. The young Sahabi said, "O Rasulullaah ﷺ! I have two wives who are much prettier than this red cheeked one (gesturing towards Hadhrat Aisha ﷺ). If you so desire, I will divorce one of them for you to marry."

Amused by the offer of this new Muslim, Hadhrat Aisha ﷺ asked him light-heartedly, "Are you better looking than your wives or are they better looking than you?"

The young man replied, "I am better looking than both of them." Later after he had left, Rasulullaah ﷺ and Hadhrat Aisha ﷺ were stilled amused at the straightforwardness of the young man. This young man's name was Hadhrat Dhahaaq ﷺ.[1]

[1] 'Mustadrak Haakim'

The knot of love

Hadhrat Aisha ﵁ narrates that after her Nikaah to Rasulullaah ﷺ, when he brought her to live with him, she asked him one day, "How much do you love me?" Rasulullaah ﷺ replied, "My love for you is so deep and strong like how the knot of a rope is tied firmly and strong."

Hadhrat Aisha ﵁ says that thereafter she used to sometimes ask Rasulullaah ﷺ, "What is the condition of the knot of your love for me?" and Rasulullaah ﷺ would smile and say, "It is still strong and no change or weakness has come into it."[1]

[1] ibid

Did you see how I saved you

Once Hadhrat Abu Bakr ﵁ went to visit Rasulullaah ﷺ but when he reached the door of Rasulullaah ﷺ, he heard Hadhrat Aisha talking to Rasulullaah ﷺ in a loud voice. This greatly angered Hadhrat Abu Bakr ﵁ and once he entered he informed Hadhrat Aisha ﵂ that he had heard the manner in which she had spoken to Rasulullaah ﷺ. **As he said this he lifted his hand to slap Hadhrat Aisha ﵂ but Rasulullaah ﷺ intervened.** After Hadhrat Abu Bakr ﵁ left, Rasulullaah ﷺ said to Hadhrat Aisha ﵂, "Did you see how I saved you otherwise you would have received a slap."[1]

[1]ibid

The incident of Ielaa

Rasulullaah lived an extremely simple and ascetic life. Sometime for months on end the fire would not be lit in the house of Rasulullaah ﷺ. The wheat and dates which Rasulullaah ﷺ had divided amongst his wives was insufficient. The blessed wives of Rasulullaah ﷺ learnt that the spoils of war had increased daily from the various victories, the Muslims had attained to such an extent that even a small portion would see to all their needs.

On one occasion Hadhrat Abu Bakr رضي الله عنه and Hadhrat Umar رضي الله عنه came to visit Rasulullaah ﷺ and found the blessed wives of Rasulullaah ﷺ seeking an increase in their monthly allowance.

Hadhrat Abu Bakr رضي الله عنه and Hadhrat Umar رضي الله عنه both warned their daughters to refrain from this demand and they both promised not to cause harm to Rasulullaah ﷺ by demanding such increases but the other wives of Rasulullaah ﷺ still remained adamant on their course.

This incident and demands had such an effect on Rasulullaah ﷺ

That he had made a promise not to go near his wives for one month.

The Munafiqeen (hypocrites) earnestly awaited such incidents and quickly spread the rumour that Rasulullaah ﷺ had divorced his wives. When this news reached the Sahabah they were greatly saddened.

When the news reached Hadhrat Umar رضي الله عنه, he immediately went to visit Rasulullaah ﷺ. Rasulullaah ﷺ was resting on a simple straw mat when Hadhrat Umar رضي الله عنه entered and the mat had left an imprint on the body of Rasulullaah ﷺ. Seeing this Hadhrat Umar رضي الله عنه was unable to control himself and with tears in his eyes asked, "O Rasulullaah ﷺ! Have you divorced your wives?" Rasulullaah ﷺ replied that nothing of the sort has occurred and on hearing this called out the Takbeer and informed all the Sahabah.

After one month had passed, then Rasulullaah ﷺ first went to visit Hadhrat Aisha رضي الله عنها, who had been counting the days in anticipation. She asked Rasulullaah ﷺ when he arrived, "Rasulullaah ﷺ you vowed to stay away for one month but only twenty-nine days have passed." Rasulullaah ﷺreplied, "Aisha! Some months have twenty-nine days."[1]

[1]'Muslim'

I only left your name out

Rasulullaah ﷺ once said to Hadhrat Aisha ؓ, "I know when you are angry with me." Hadhrat Aisha ؓ enquired how Rasulullaah ﷺ was able to recognise when she was angry. Rasulullaah ﷺ replied, "When you are pleased with me you say, "O Rabb of Muhammed ﷺ" and when you are angry with me you say, "O Rabb of Ibraheem عليه السلام" Hadhrat Aisha ؓ replied, "O Rasulullaah ﷺ! You are right but even in my anger I only leave your name out (you don't leave my heart)."[1]

Allaamah Kirmaani رحمة الله عليه was written on the authority of Qaadhi Ayyaadh رحمة الله عليه that Hadhrat Aisha ؓ left the name of Rasulullaah ﷺ out on account of her modesty and there is nothing wrong with that. In addition Hadhrat Aisha ؓ saying, "I only leave your name out" is proof that even in her anger her heart was still filled with love for Rasulullaah ﷺ. Leaving the name of Rasulullaah ﷺ out was a result of natural tendency, which women normally do with those whom they have intense love for.[2]

[1]'Bukhaari', 'Muslim'
[2]'Bukhaari'

Before the Battle of Jamal

Hadhrat Aisha ﷺ had departed to perform Hajj, accompanied by Hadhrat Umie Salamah ﷺ and Hadhrat Safiyyah ﷺ, when they learned of the rebellion against Hadhrat Uthmaan ﷺ and his martyrdom. They were greatly saddened by this news and concerned by the division and discord that would result because of it. It was during this same time that Hadhrat Zubair ﷺ, Hadhrat Talha ﷺ, Hadhrat Nu'maan bin Basheer ﷺ, Hadhrat Ka'ab bin Ajazah ﷺ and a few other Sahabah arrived in Makkah after fleeing from Madinah, as the murderers of Hadhrat Uthmaan ﷺ had intentions of murdering them as well. These Sahabah were in opposition to the insurgents and were endeavouring to put an end to the turmoil they had created.

When they reached Makkah, they sought council with Hadhrat Aisha ﷺ as to the way forward. Hadhrat Aisha ﷺ gave them the following advice, "Do not return to Madinah until the people have rallied behind Hadhrat Ali ﷺ, who has been prevented from avenging the blood of Uthmaan ﷺ as this will only increase the turmoil at this moment. In the interim you should go to such a place where you will be safe until Ameerul-Mu'mineen is able to regain control of the state. Do whatever you can to remove these insurgents from around Ameerul-Mu'mineen, thus granting him the ability to avenge the blood of Uthmaan ﷺ.

These Sahabah accepted the council of Hadhrat Aisha and intended to travel to Basra, as the Islaamic armies were encamped in Basra. When they intended to leave for Basra, they asked Hadhrat Aisha to also remain with them in Basra until peace is restored.

The inability of Hadhrat Ali to avenge the blood of Hadhrat Uthmaan by executing his murderers has been established from narrations in 'Nahjul Balaaghah'. One should bear in mind that 'Nahjul Balaaghah' is considered to be one of the most reliable and trustworthy books according to the Shias. It is mentioned in 'Nahjul Balaaghah', "A few of Ameerul Mu'mineen Hadhrat Ali's companions suggested to him that it would be better if he avenged the blood of Uthmaan by executing his murderers. Hadhrat Ali replied, "My brothers! I am not unaware of what you say but how do I accomplish this when these very people have taken control of Madinah and your slaves as well and the surrounding Arabs all support them. If I issue the order for their execution now, how will it be carried out?"

Hadhrat Aisha was aware of the inability of Hadhrat Ali on one hand and on the other she was also aware of the pain the murder of Hadhrat Uthmaan had inflicted on the hearts of the Muslims and that the longer Hadhrat Ali took in executing his murderers the turmoil would only increase. In addition the murderers of Hadhrat Uthmaan would participate in the gatherings of Hadhrat Ali.

Those who were unaware of the inability of Hadhrat Ali had misgivings regarding Hadhrat Ali and these misgivings regarding Hadhrat Ali could possibly lead to another rebellion. Therefore in order to calm to matters down; advising people to remain patient and to strengthen the authority of Hadhrat Ali as well put an end to the division between the

Muslims and reconcile between them, Hadhrat Aisha ﷺ decided to travel to Basra. **Accompanied by her Mahram nephew, Hadhrat Abdullaah bin Zubair ﷺ (who was the son of her sister, Hadhrat Asmaa ﷺ)** and others she travelled to Basra, the purpose of which she later clarified before Hadhrat Qa'qaa ﷺ.

In a time of such great division the importance of reconciliation between the believers is apparent. Therefore if Hadhrat Aisha ﷺ travelled to Basra, accompanied by her Mahram (blood relations) and in the confines of her carriage, what justification can the Shias have for their argument that Hadhrat Aisha ﷺ acted against the laws of the Quraan?[1]

[1] 'Qasas Ma'aariful Quraan'

Battle of Jamal

Hadhrat Aisha ﷺ was still in Makkah, after having performed Hajj, when she received the horrific news of the martyrdom of Hadhrat Uthmaan ﷺ. Hadhrat Aisha ﷺ had intended to return to Madinah in Muharram after Umrah but after having performed Umrah and reaching Sarf, she met Hadhrat Ubaid bin Abi Salamah who informed her, "Are you not aware that Hadhrat Uthmaan ﷺ has been martyred and Madinah remained without a Khalifah for eight days?" Hadhrat Aisha ﷺ enquired as to what the people had done thereafter, on which she was informed that the people of Madinah had pledged their allegiance to Hadhrat Ali ﷺ and that the insurgents still maintain control over Madinah.

Hadhrat Aisha returned to Makkah after hearing this news and entered the Masjid Haraam. She entered the Hateem and people sealed the area off with a screen. After everyone had gathered, Hadhrat Aisha ﷺ addressed them all saying,

"O people! The rebels, slaves and troublemakers from various cities and towns haveaccused Hadhrat Uthmaan ﷺof being unjust and crating turmoil; that he had appointed such a young governor whose teeth have not yet grown, even though he had been used previously (for other duties of the state) and protected them as well. These are such matters which had occurred previously as well and which could only be rectified by this youngster. However those bent on creating trouble pursued him, intending to usurp his right. They portray themselves to be seeking justice but when they could not prove him to be at fault, they resorted to rebellion and mutiny. In this manner people have been misinformed by their claims and assertions. In addition they have spilled the very blood which Allaah Ta'ala has forbidden to spill. They have committed murder in the same city which Allaah Ta'ala has made the home of His Rasul ﷺ.They have committed murder in the same month wherein Allaah Ta'ala has forbidden bloodshed. They have plundered the very wealth which Allaah Ta'ala has forbidden them to take. The month in which the blood of even the disbelievers is safe, which Allaah Ta'ala has granted honour, the blood of Uthmaan ؓ was made Halaal to spill and the sacredness of this month was dishonoured."

"I take an oath by Allaah! Even if the entire earth were to be filled with people of the likes of the murderers of Uthmaan ؓ then too one finger of Uthmaan ؓ is superior to them all. In this gathering today I seek your assistance against these rebels, so that they may be punished accordingly."

After this speech, Hadhrat Aisha ؓ mounted her camel named Askar, which had been purchased by Ya'alah bin Umayyah for eighty Dinaars, and preparations were made for the army.

Hadhrat Ali ؓ was informed of the preparation of this army. He appointed Hadhrat Sahal bin Haneef Ansaari in charge of Madinah and set out to confront this army.

The trouble and turmoil which arise during times of division and conflict is not hidden from any intelligent person and in every age there have been those waiting to exploit such circumstances. **They use these misunderstandings between the Muslims against them causing them to quarrel, fight and even kill each other.** Here too this occurred and the Munafiqeen and insurgents portrayed the journey of Hadhrat Aisha ﷺ to Basra with the Sahabah of Madinah to be in opposition of Hadhrat Ali ﷺ. They insisted upon Hadhrat Ali ﷺ that if he is indeed the Ameerul-Mu'mineen then he should proceed and put an end to this rebellion.

Sahabah such as Hadhrat Hasan ﷺ, Hadhrat Hussein ﷺ, Hadhrat Abdullaah bin Ja'far ﷺ, Hadhrat Abdullaah bin Abbaas ﷺ disagreed with this opinion and advised that Hadhrat Ali ﷺ should not march upon them until the truth has been established. However the opposition outnumbered them and Hadhrat Ali ﷺ was inclined towards them. Hadhrat Ali then sat out from Madinah also accompanied by these rebels.

Hadhrat Ali ﷺ reached the area of Rabthah, when he was informed that the army of Hadhrat Aisha ﷺhad passed them. Hadhrat Ali ﷺremained encamped here until receiving the next message.

Urfie relates that they were marching with Hadhrat Aisha ﷺuntil they reached the wells of Haw'aab, where dogs began barking at them. People asked him where they were and he replied, "These wells are known as the wells of Haw'aab."

Urfie narrates that when Hadhrat Aisha ﷺ heard this then she desired to return saying that Rasulullaah ﷺ once addressed his blessed wives saying, **"What will occur when the dogs of Haw'aab will begin barking at one of you? (Indicating that a calamity would befall thereafter)"** Hadhrat Aisha ﷺ then insisted on returning and turned her camel around. People also followed her until the next day Hadhrat Abdullaah bin Zubair arrived and extremely apprehensive said, "The army of Ali is in pursuit of you."

Hadhrat Aisha ؓ and those with her then advanced and reached the area of Mureed, which they entered and encamped. Uthmaan bin Haneef proceeded with his soldiers to stop them. Hadhrat Talha ؓ advanced and addressed them; praising Allaah and enumerating the virtues of Hadhrat Uthmaan ؓ and the events of his martyrdom. Hadhrat Aisha ؓ then addressed them in an eloquent manner, befitting the situation at that time, the result of which was that the companions of Uthmaan bin Haneef broke away from him. The following morning a battle broke out which continued with much ferocity. Many of Uthmaan bin Haneef's companions were slain in this battle and both parties suffered many injuries. Hadhrat Aisha ؓ called on them to refrain from battle but the opposition did not comply and continued to fight until all of them were slain.

The army of Uthmaan bin Haneef was defeated and those that remained sought sanctuary, which they were granted. Thereafter Uthmaan bin Haneef was imprisoned and some of those who had participated in rebellion of Hadhrat Uthmaan ؓ.

Hadhrat Ali was encamped at Dhi-Qaar at this time, when he called upon Hadhrat Qa'qaa bin Umar to proceed to Hadhrat Aisha ؓ as his messenger and find a means to reconcile. Hadhrat Qa'qaa ؓ reached the camp of Hadhrat Aisha ؓ and enquired the reason for their arrival in Basra. **She replied that her purpose is only reconciliation between the Muslims. He then called for Hadhrat Talha ؓ and Hadhrat Zubair ؓ and enquired the purpose of them coming to Basra and they replied that desired nothing more than justice to be exacted from the murderers of Uthmaan ؓ.**

Hadhrat Qa'qaa bin Amr replied that they had already killed six hundred of the rebels and further battle would only cause more destruction. **He said that in order for justice to be meted out, stability had to be established first and this could only be acquired if the Muslims unite once again.** "After this has been established then we will be able to exact justice for Hadhrat Uthmaan's ﷺ murder" Hadhrat Qa'qaa ﷺ said. He added, "Therefore it is incumbent upon you all adopt peace." Hadhrat Talha ﷺ and Hadhrat Zubair ﷺ both replied that they were willing to do so if this was the intention of Hadhrat Ali ﷺ.

Hadhrat Qa'qaa ﷺ returned to Hadhrat Ali and informed him of what had transpired which brought him great joy and after announcing the peace treaty, slept that night peacefully. Both parties had decided to return and the next three days were spent in preparation for departure, with all having complete conviction that there would now be peace. **On the fourth day it was to be announced that Hadhrat Ali ﷺ was going to meet with Hadhrat Talha ﷺ and Hadhrat Zubair ﷺ.**

However the murderers of Hadhrat Uthmaan ﷺ spent the entire night in anguish, discussing ways to save their lives. **They all came to the decision that they have to start the war in order to save their own lives. They decided that the following morning, at first light, they would launch an attack on the armies of Hadhrat Aisha ﷺ, and they would attack in return, thinking that Hadhrat Ali ﷺ had betrayed them.**

These devils set out in secret the next morning to fulfil their plans, each hiding amongst their own tribes. They launched a sudden attack and the battle field was set ablaze with the clanging of swords and fierce battle. Each party called its supporters to come to their aid and thinking that they were betrayed by Hadhrat Ali ﷺ, Hadhrat Aisha ﷺ and her supporters advanced into battle.

The agents of Ibn Sabaa were spurring the battle on and when Hadhrat Ali ﷺ witnessed what was transpiring, he urged people to lower their swords and to abstain from fighting but after seeing that the battle was impossible to stop he marched forward as well.

Ka'ab bin Thour advised Hadhrat Aisha ﷺ to advance into the battlefield, suggesting that peace may be acquired by her presence. Hadhrat Aisha ﷺ then proceeded into the battlefield with the hope of preventing further bloodshed.

The battle was fierce and on seeing this Hadhrat Aisha ﷺ asked Hadhrat Ka'ab to bring a Quraan and invited the people to act upon the Quraan. Hadhrat Ka'ab brought a Quraan and as he passed the opposition, led by the henchmen of Ibn Sabaa who desired nothing war, they prevented him from proceeding.

Hadhrat Ali ﷺ was at the back of the army and he understood that the opposition were not prepared for anything but war. When Ka'ab presented the Quraan before the agents of Ibn Sabaa, they attacked him and martyred him. They then made the camel of Hadhrat Aisha ﷺ there target and began raining arrows upon it.

When the people of Basra saw that Hadhrat Aisha ﷺ was their only target, they surrounded her camel and defended her. The battle continued into the afternoon and stopped for Zuhr Salaah but began again thereafter.

The army of Hadhrat Ali ﷺ was gaining headway in the battle and he ordered the camel of Hadhrat Aisha ﷺ to be killed as this would cause them to scatter and the battle to end. As a result the camel of Hadhrat Aisha ﷺ was killed.

Hadhrat Ali ordered Muhammed bin Abu Bakr to erect a tent around the camel of Hadhrat Aisha and ensure that she has not been injured.

Hadhrat Ali then gave sanctuary to the army of Hadhrat Aisha and in this manner the battle ended. Hadhrat Ali ordered that Hadhrat Aisha should be taken to safety in Basra and was accompanied by Muhammed bin Abu Bakr and Hadhrat Ammaar bin Yaasir, where she stayed at the home of Abdullaah bin Khalaf Khuzaa'ie. Hadhrat Ali stayed for three days in the battlefield as people buried the deceased.

Hadhrat Aisha desired to return to Makkah, so Hadhrat Ali provided her with the provisions required for the journey. As Hadhrat Aisha was leaving Hadhrat Ali stood in honour of her in which Hadhrat Aisha addressed everyone saying, "My sons! We stood against each other in haste in future let not our differences prompt us to stand against each other. I take an oath by Allaah! **IfI had any difference with Ali then this differences were like that of a mother-in-law with her son-in-law. In my opinion Ali is a pious person."**

Hadhrat Ali then addressed everyone and said, "O people! I take an oath by Allaah! Ummul Mu'mineen has spoken the truth. Our difference was indeed of this sort. **Hadhrat Aisha is the wife of your Nabi in this world and Aakhirah.**

After this address, Hadhrat Ali accompanied Hadhrat Aisha on foot for a number of miles and the ordered his sons, Hadhrat Hasan and Hadhrat Hussein, to accompany Hadhrat Aisha on her journey.

In essence as a result of the mischief and deceit of the hypocrites two revered groups of the Muslims fought each other, and at the end of the battle both parties were grieved by the outcome.

Whenever Hadhrat Aisha ﵂ would remember the accounts of that day, she would begin weeping so profusely that her entire scarf would become wet with tears. Similarly Hadhrat Ali ﵁ would also grieve whenever he thought of the events of this battle. After the battle as Hadhrat Ali ﵁ gazed at the fallen of that day, he hit his thigh and said, "If only I had died and been forgotten before this."

In some narrations it is mentioned that whenever Hadhrat Aisha ﵂ would read the verse , "Remain in your homes" (Surah Ahzaab) then she would begin weeping.

The reason for her weeping was not because she felt that it was impermissible for her to have left her home or that it was a sin to do so but her weeping was on account of the incident that had transpired and the losses suffered when she had left her home.[1]

[1]'Ruhul Ma'aani', 'Taareekh Thabri', 'Taareekh Ibn Katheer' on the authority of 'Ma'aariful Quraan'

Tahreem

The life of Rasulullaah ﷺ was a sterling example of justice and equality. This is the reason why in every aspect of Rasulullaah's life one will see exemplary acts of justice, equality and fairness.

Just as Rasulullaah ﷺ was fair in other parts of his life so too was he just and equal in his married life. Rasulullaah's ﷺ entire married life was one of fairness; meeting out like treatment to all of his spouses such that if a person were to search out even one instance of injustice, he would fail to find it.

It was the habit of Rasulullaah ﷺ that after Asr Salaah he would visit all of his wives and enquire about them, after which he would return. This was the case for all of his wives.

It just so happened that on a few occasions he took longer than usual when visiting Hadhrat Zainab ﵂ while his other wives remained waiting to be visited in the normal time. When Hadhrat Aisha ﵂ enquired as to the reason for Rasulullaah's ﷺ delay she discovered that Hadhrat Zainab ﵂ had been gifted a bottle of honey by one of her relatives and since Rasulullaah ﷺ loved honey very much, she would offer it to Rasulullaah ﷺ, which is why he was delayed every day.

How was it possible for the wives of Rasulullaah ﷺ to endure the delay in seeing Rasulullaah ﷺ when every moment spent in his company was more beloved to them than the entire universe? As a result Hadhrat Aisha ؓ informed Hadhrat Hafsah ؓ and Hadhrat Saudah ؓ and together they thought of a plan to put an end to this.

Rasulullaah ﷺ abhorred bad odours. Honey usually has the taste and fragrance of the flower from which the bees extract nectar. Maghaafeer is a type of flower native to Arabia, which has a bad odour and when bees make honey from this flower then the honey has its odour as well.

Now Hadhrat Aisha ؓ, Hadhrat Hafsah ؓ, and Hadhrat Saudah ؓ devised the plan that when Rasulullaah ﷺ will come to visit them then they will each enquire about the odour emanating from the mouth of Rasulullaah ﷺand when he replies that he has had honey then they will say, "Perhaps it has been made from Maghaafeer"

This is exactly what occurred and Rasulullaah ﷺ said that he had eaten honey and the wives replied that perhaps the bees made the honey from the Maghafeer flower. Since Rasulullaah ﷺ disliked those things that give of an odour, he took an oath that he will never drink honey again. Not desiring to sadden Hadhrat Zainab ؓ, Rasulullaah ﷺ instructed them to keep his oath a secret. Allaah Ta'ala then revealed the reality of this incident to His Nabi ﷺ, in the following verse,

"O Nabi ﷺ! In seeking the pleasure of your wives, why do you declare unlawful that which Allaah has made lawful for you? Allaah is Most Forgiving, Most Merciful." (Surah Tahreem: 1)

Those who do not wear old clothes do not deserve to wear new clothes

Hadhrat Katheer bin Ubaid رحمة الله عليه narrates that he came to visit Hadhrat Aisha رضي الله عنها when she said to him, "Let me finish patching my clothes then I will listen to what you have to say."

He said, "O Ummul Mu'mineen! If I were to inform people that the mother of the believers is patching her clothes then they will see this as a sign of miserliness."

Hadhrat Aisha رضي الله عنها replied, "Do what you like! Those who do not wear old clothes do not deserve to wear new clothes." Which means that those who do not wear old clothes in this world will not wear new clothes in the Aakhirah.[1]

[1] 'Hayaatus Sahabah', 'Bukhaari'

Hadhrat Aisha listens to a poem

Hadhrat Aisha ﷺ narrates that Rasulullaah ﷺ came to visit her one day when two girls of the Ansaar were reciting poetry to her, which the Ansaar used to recite in battle. When Rasulullaah ﷺ arrived he rested on the bed and turned his face the other way. Just then Hadhrat Abu Bakr ﷺ arrived and scolded her saying, "Such behaviour before Rasulullaah ﷺ!" Indicating that they should refrain from it.

Rasulullaah ﷺ instructed Hadhrat Abu Bakr ﷺ to leave them and when Hadhrat Abu Bakr ﷺ was busy with something else, Hadhrat Aisha ﷺ instructed the girls to leave.[1]

[1]'Bukhaari'

Rasulullaah ﷺ consoles Hadhrat Aisha

Hadhrat Aisha ﷺ has accompanied Rasulullaah ﷺ on the farewell Hajj and when Rasulullaah ﷺ intended to don his Ihraam, she applied perfume on Rasulullaah ﷺ. Later when they reached the area of Sarf, Hadhrat Aisha's ﷺ cycle began. When Rasulullaah ﷺ came to see Hadhrat Aisha ﷺ he found her weeping. Rasulullaah ﷺ consoled her saying, "Allaah Ta'ala has decreed this for all the daughters of Hadhrat Aadam عليه السلام (thus there is no reason to cry and as far as Hajj is concerned), you may perform all the rites of Hajj except for Tawaaf, which you can perform once you attain purity."[1]

[1] 'Bukhaari', 'Abu Dawood', 'Nasaai'

Takhyeer

Hadhrat Jaabir ﷺ narrates that the blessed wives of Rasulullaah ﷺ once all requested an increase in their allowance from Rasulullaah ﷺ. They said, "The wives of Caesar and Khusroe are adorned with various jewels and have thousands of servants at their call and you are well-aware of our poverty, so please increase our allowance for us."

Rasulullaah ﷺ was saddened by the desire of his blessed wives to be treated in the same luxurious manner as the wives of the Caesar and Khusroe as they had not yet understood the value of being in the house of Rasulullaah ﷺ. They did not understand that their request was hurting the feelings of Rasulullaah ﷺ. Allaah Ta'ala then revealed the following verses, which came to be known as 'Ayaat Takhyeer',

"O Nabi ﷺ! Say to your wives, "If you desire the life of this world and its adornments, then come forward. I shall grant you a generous provision and separate from you *(divorce you)* in a cordial manner. However, if you desire Allaah, His Rasul and the home of the Aakhirah, then *(you may continue enjoying the status of being his wives and living with the allowance he provides because)* Allaah has certainly prepared a grand reward for those of you who do good deeds."

(Surah Ahzaab: 28,29)

Hadhrat Aisha ﵂ narrates that when this verse was revealed then Rasulullaah ﷺ first announced it to her and before reciting it to her said, "Do not be hasty in replying to it but rather discuss it with your parents first."

Hadhrat Aisha ﵂ narrates, "Rasulullaah ﷺ told me to discuss it with my parents before replying because he was sure that my parents would never advise me to separate from Rasulullaah ﷺ."

Hadhrat Aisha replied when hearing this verse, "What? Do I still need to discuss this with my parents? I choose Allaah, His Rasul and the home of the Aakhirah."

When Rasulullaah ﷺ heard this, his happiness gleamed from his face and the other wives of Rasulullaah ﷺ also gave the same reply and none of them were prepared to accept the luxuries of this world over Rasulullaah ﷺ.[1]

[1]'Bukhaari'

Hadhrat Aisha's desire to have children

One day Rasulullaah ﷺ came to visit Hadhrat Aisha ﷺ along with his son, Hadhrat Ibraheem ﷺ. Rasulullaah ﷺ called Hadhrat Aisha ﷺ, so that she could see the resemblance between them. Seeing this Hadhrat Aisha's ﷺ heart desired, "O Allaah! Let me also give birth to the children of Rasulullaah ﷺ so that he will love me even more and my status will increase in his eyes above that of his other wives." With this thought in her mind, she felt like crying but contained her tears. Rasulullaah ﷺ understood this from her manner and was not pleased.[1]

[1]'Qasasun Nisaa fil Quraan'

Hadhrat Aisha's common name

A common name is a sign of honour amongst the Arabs, which is why every person was usually addressed by their common names. Since Hadhrat Aisha رضي الله عنها had no children, she also did not have a common name. When her nephew Hadhrat Abdullaah bin Zubair رضي الله عنه was born, she brought him to Rasulullaah ﷺ. Rasulullaah ﷺ placed his saliva in the mouth of the baby and this was the first thing to go in to the stomach of the child after he was born.

Hadhrat Aisha رضي الله عنها said to Rasulullaah ﷺ, "All your other wives have common names, so please grant me a common name as well." Rasulullaah ﷺ replied, "Take the name of your nephew." Hadhrat Aisha رضي الله عنها then kept her common name Umie Abdullaah, which remained until her demise.[1]

[1]'Tirmidhi', 'Ma'aariful Quraan'

Rasulullaah ﷺ donates a Dinaar in his final illness

Hadhrat Aisha narrates that Rasulullaah ﷺ once ordered her during his final illness to give in charity the Dinaar that he had in his home. She relates that she was concerned about his illness so did not fulfil his order right away. Later when Rasulullaah ﷺ was feeling a little better, he enquired from her as to whether she had given the Dinaar away or not. Hadhrat Aisha relied that she had been busy tending to him during his illness (because of which she had not given it in charity). Rasulullaah ﷺ then ordered the Dinaar to be brought to him and when it was handed over to him he said, **"What will happen to Muhammed ﷺ ifhe meets his Rabb in this condition that he still has a Dinaar in his possession." And immediately gave it in charity.**[1]

[1]'Musnad Ahmed'

Bequest for Hadhrat Abu Bakr to be Khalifah

Hadhrat Aisha narrates that she once complained of headache saying, "Oh my head!" on which Rasulullaah replied, "I should actually say O! My head"

Rasulullaah said, during his final illness, "I had intended to call upon Abu Bakr and his son (Abdur Rahmaan bin Abu Bakr so that I could make a bequest), so that those who concoct ideas may not do so and those who are desirous (of position) may not desire but (I abandoned this because) I thought to myself that Allaah Ta'ala and the Muslims will allow any other person to be Khalifah but Abu Bakr (thus I abandoned my intention)."[1]

[1] 'Bukhaari'

A unique honour

When Rasulullaah's ﷺ final illness began he was residing in the house of Hadhrat Maymoonah ﵄ and when his health began to deteriorate further day by day then Rasulullaah ﷺ sought permission from his other wives to spend these days of his illness in the house of Hadhrat Aisha ﵄. **The blessed wives of Rasulullaah ﷺ all agreed and Rasulullaah ﷺ was taken to the house of Hadhrat Aisha ﵄ by Hadhrat Ali ﵁ and Hadhrat Fadhl bin Abbaas ﵁.**This was where Rasulullaah ﷺ then passed away and this was where Rasulullaah ﷺwas then buried.[1]

[1]'Bukhaari'

Hadhrat Abu Bakr makes Imaamat

Hadhrat Aisha narrates that when Rasulullaah was in his final illness and his ill health increased; one morning the believers were awaiting Rasulullaah to lead them in Fajr Salaah. Rasulullaah had tried repeatedly to stand up but was unable to do so, falling unconscious on each attempt. **Finally Rasulullaah ordered, "Instruct Abu Bakr to lead the Salaah."** Hadhrat Aisha narrates that she thought that whoever will be appointed to stand in the place of Rasulullaah will not be welcomed by the people thus is I said, "O Rasulullaah! Abu Bakr is a soft hearted man and he will be unable to fulfil this task. He will begin to weep (and will therefore be unable to fulfil the duty of Imaamat)." However Rasulullaah still insisted that Hadhrat Abu Bakr should lead the Salaah even after hearing this. Hadhrat Aisha then approached Hadhrat Hafsah and asked her to speak to Rasulullaah. When she made the same request to **Rasulullaah, he replied, "You women are like the ones who deceived Hadhrat Yusuf. Instruct Abu Bakr to lead the Salaah."** Hadhrat Abu Bakr then led the Salaah and the Sahabah followed him in their Salaah."[1]

[1] 'Bukhaari'

A great virtue of Hadhrat Aisha

The illness of Rasulullaah ﷺ had increased and Rasulullaah ﷺ was about to leave this world. Hadhrat Aisha رضي الله عنها was sitting alongside Rasulullaah ﷺ and he was leaning on her. During this time, Hadhrat Aisha's brother, Hadhrat Abdur Rahmaan bin Abu Bakr رضي الله عنه, entered and he happened to be using the Miswaak. Rasulullaah ﷺ stared towards his Miswaak and since Hadhrat Aisha رضي الله عنها was well acquainted with the habits of Rasulullaah ﷺ, she understood that he desired to use the Miswaak. **Hadhrat Aisha then took the Miswaak from her brother and after softening it with her teeth gave it to Rasulullaah ﷺ, who accepted it and made Miswaak of his teeth.** Hadhrat Aisha رضي الله عنها used to often proudly say, "From all the blessed wives of Rasulullaah ﷺ, I am the only one who had the honour of having her had saliva touch the blessed mouth of Rasulullaah ﷺ.[1]

[1] 'Muslim', 'Tirmidhi'

Rasulullaah ﷺ passes away in the lap of Hadhrat Aisha

Hadhrat Aisha ﷺ was supplicating to Allaah Ta'ala to cure Rasulullaah ﷺ when he suddenly grabbed the hand of Hadhrat Aisha ﷺ, since he was sleeping in her lap, and said, "O Allaah! The greatest friend!"

Hadhrat Aisha ﷺ narrates that Rasulullaah ﷺ used to say when he was still in good health that the **Ambiyaa are given the choice between life in this world or in the Aakhirah in their final moments.** Thus as soon as Hadhrat Aisha ﷺ heard Rasulullaah ﷺ utter these words she knew that Rasulullaah ﷺ had chosen the life of the Aakhirah.

She asked Rasulullaah, "Are you in severe pain, O Rasulullaah ﷺ!" and Rasulullaah ﷺ replied, "Reward is in accordancewith the pain (that is the more pain one endures the greater the reward will be in the Aakhirah)."

Until this point in time Hadhrat Aisha ﷺ was still holding Rasulullaah ﷺ she says, "I suddenly felt the weight of Rasulullaah's ﷺ body pressing against me and when looked towards him, I saw that his eyes were open. Gently I rested Rasulullaah ﷺ on the pillow and began to weep." Later Rasulullaah ﷺ was buried in the same room of Hadhrat Aisha ﷺ.[1]

[1]'Bukhaari'

Three wisdoms from one advice

Ibn Abi Saa'ib Taabi'ie was an orator of Madinah. It is the habit of some orators, in order to spur up their audience recite rhyming supplications, and remain ever ready to show off their ability before the masses. Hadhrat Aisha ﷺ once addressed him saying, "Praise three things or I will absolve myself from you." He enquired what these three things were and she replied, "Do not rhyme your supplications because Rasulullaah ﷺ and his companions did not do so. Lecture only once a week and if you do not agree to this then only twice a week and if this too is not possible then three times only. Do not separate people from the book of Allaah, it must not be that you begin giving your lecture wherever people are gathered, cutting of their speech but only talk when they request you to."[1]

[1]'Musnad Ahmed'

Impartiality

Generally it is very difficult to find people who are impartial but those individuals who were taught by Rasulullaah ﷺ were endowed with this quality, which is why they were still able to remain united despite their differences in personality. Hadhrat Aisha رضي الله عنها was also blessed with this unique quality of impartiality.

On one occasion a person from Egypt came to visit Hadhrat Aisha رضي الله عنها. Hadhrat Aisha رضي الله عنها asked him about the exploits of the current governor of Egypt. The Egyptian replied, "We do not see any point of criticism in him; if a person's camel dies he gives them a new one, if one does not possess a servant then he grants them one and if one is in need then he fulfils their need."

Hadhrat Aisha replied, "Despite the ill treatment he showed to my brother, Muhammed bin Abu Bakr رضي الله عنه, I will not abstain from informing you of something. Rasulullaah ﷺ was in my home when he made the following supplication, "whoever is a governor over my Ummat; if he is severe on them then You be severe on him and if he is kind to them You be kind to him."[1]

[1]'Muslim'

Hadhrat Aisha's anger at her nephew

Hadhrat Abdullaah bin Zubair ﷺ was an esteemed companion of Rasulullaah ﷺ and was the nephew of Hadhrat Aisha ﷺ. Hadhrat Aisha ﷺ was very kind, affectionate and generous towards him and it was as if she had raised him.

Hadhrat Abdullaah bin Zubair ﷺ was concerned about the generous and lavish spending of Hadhrat Aisha ﷺthat she remains in difficulty but whatever she received she immediately gives it in charity. It was on account of this that Hadhrat Abdullaah bin Zubair ﷺ once said that they need to restrain the hand of Hadhrat Aisha (to prevent her from giving excess charity).

When Hadhrat Aisha ﷺ was informed about the statement of her nephew, she became extremely angry with him and took an oath not to speak to him.

Hadhrat Abdullaah bin Zubair ﷺ was distressed by the anger of his aunt and sent many people to plead for forgiveness on his behalf but to no avail and Hadhrat Aisha ﷺ refused to break her oath. **Eventually Hadhrat Abdullah bin Zubair ﷺcould no longer contain himself and accompanied by Hadhrat Hasan ﷺ and Hadhrat Hussein ﷺ he went before Hadhrat Aisha ﷺ.**

The two grandsons took permission and entered the house of Hadhrat Aisha and Hadhrat Abdullaah bin Zubair snuck in with them. Once they sat and began talking with Hadhrat Aisha from behind the veil, Hadhrat Abdullaah bin Zubair snuck behind the veil and clutching his aunt he began weeping and begging for forgiveness. Hadhrat Hasan and Hadhrat Hussein also pleaded on his behalf, reminding her of Rasulullaah's prohibition of abstaining from speaking to another.

Hadhrat Aisha when reminded of these Ahaadeeth began crying and forgave Hadhrat Abdullaah bin Zubair. In recompense for breaking her oath she continued to set slaves free until she had set forty slaves free. Later whenever she remembered the oath she had broken, she would begin weeping until her scarf would become wet with tears.[1]

[1] 'Bukhaari'

Hadhrat Aisha speaks candidly

Amr bin Ghaalib Taabi'ie رحمة الله عليه narrates that he went to visit Hadhrat Aisha رضي الله عنها along with Hadhrat Ammaar and Ashtar. Hadhrat Ammaar greeted Hadhrat Aisha رضي الله عنها who replied, "Peace be upon those who follow the path of guidance." Hadhrat Ammaar repeated his greeting three times after which he said, "Even if you do not like it, you are our mother." Hadhrat Aisha رضي الله عنها then enquired who was accompanying him, to which Hadhrat Ammaar replied that it is Ashtar. Hadhrat Aisha رضي الله عنها asked, "Are you the same person who intended to kill my nephew (i.e. Hadhrat Abdullaah bin Zubair رضي الله عنه)?" Ashtar replied thathe did indeed intend to kill Hadhrat Abdullaah bin Zubair رضي الله عنه. Hadhrat Aisha رضي الله عنها replied, "Were you to have killed him then you would never attain success. Ammaar! Did you not hear Rasulullaah ﷺ say, "The blood of a Muslim is not permissible to spill except in three circumstances; if a person commits adultery, a person abandons Islaam after embracing it and if a person is executed for committing murder."[1]

[1]'Bukhaari', 'Muslim', 'Tirmidhi'

Watching the Abyssinians play

Hadhrat Aisha narrates that she saw Rasulullaah standing at the door of her house, watching the Abyssinians play with their spears in the courtyard of the Masjid. Rasulullaah enshrouded Hadhrat Aisha with his shawl, and placing her chin on the shoulder of Rasulullaah she also watched the Abyssinians play. Rasulullaah continued to stand with her until Hadhrat Aisha grew tired and returned to the house.[1]

In the narrations reported by Hadhrat Ubaid bin Umair Laithi Taabi'ie it is mentioned that Hadhrat Aisha said, "I desired to watch the Abyssinians playing with their spears, so Rasulullaah stood in front of Hadhrat Aisha and they watched the spectacle.[2]

Allaamah Sindhi mentioned regarding this incident that Hadhrat Aisha only desired to witness the method in which they practiced and did not look at their faces and that this incident occurred before the prohibition of looking towards men was revealed.[3]

[1]'Bukhaari', 'Muslim', 'Nasaai'
[2]'Musnad Ahmed'
[3]'Haashia Sindhi, Nasaai Shareef'

Two silver bangles

It is impermissible according to the laws of Shari'ah for a man to use gold and silk but it is permissible for a woman to use them. However since Rasulullaah ﷺ disliked such luxuries and lavishness in his home and his gaze remained ever fixed on the life of the Aakhirah when Hadhrat Aisha once wore two gold bangles, he said to her, "Aisha! Should I not tell you of two bangles even better then the one's you are wearing; have two silver bangles made and add the colour of saffron to it."[1]

[1] 'Nasaai'

An incident one night

On night Hadhrat Zainab came to visit Hadhrat Aisha ; during those days there never use to be a lamp in the home. At the same time Rasulullaah also arrived and stood alongside one of them. Hadhrat Aisha immediately said that it was Hadhrat Zainab he was standing next to. Hadhrat Zainab was annoyed by this and immediately began arguing with Hadhrat Aisha and Hadhrat Aisha returned her comments. Hadhrat Abu Bakr happened to be standing outside the Masjid and asked Rasulullaah to meet him outside. Rasulullaah stepped outside and sensing her father's anger with her, she immediately kept silent.[1]

[1]'Tafseerul Um'

Virtue of raising children

Hadhrat Aisha narrates that one day a woman came to visit her and asked her a question. She was accompanied by her two young daughters. Hadhrat Aisha only had one date in her possession at that time, which she gave to the mother.

The mother took the date and broke it into two; giving each child half and taking nothing for herself. As the women left Rasulullaah arrived and Hadhrat Aisha informed him of the entire incident. Rasulullaah said, "That person (man or woman) who has been burdened with the upbringing ofgirls, i.e. the responsibility of raising and providing for them has been placed on his shoulders, and he treats them kindly then these girls will be a barrier and obstruction between him and the fire of Jahannam."[1]

[1]'Bukhaari', 'Muslim'

Her status in knowledge

Allaah Ta'ala blessed Hadhrat Aisha رضي الله عنها with a lofty status in the field of knowledge such that eminent Sahabah and Taabi'een would refer to her. On one occasion Hadhrat Athiyah رحمة الله عليه and Hadhrat Masrooq رحمة الله عليه came to see Hadhrat Aisha رضي الله عنها. They asked her, "O Ummul Mu'mineen! There are two companions of Rasulullaah صلى الله عليه وسلم; one breaks his fast immediately and performs his Salaah as soon as the time sets in and the other delays breaking his fast and the performance of his Salaah (so which of the two is a better practice?)."

Hadhrat Aisha رضي الله عنها enquired, "Who does not delay?" they replied that it was Hadhrat Abdullaah bin Mas'ood رضي الله عنه who breaks his fast immediately and performs his Salaah immediately when the time sets in. Hadhrat Aisha رضي الله عنها replied, "I saw Rasulullaah صلى الله عليه وسلم doing exactly like this (i.e. not delaying in breaking his fast and performing his Salaah)."[1]

[1]'Tirmidhi', Nasaai'

Advice to Hadhrat Muawiyah رضی اللہ عنہ

Hadhrat Muawiyah ﷺ wrote a letter to Hadhrat Aisha ﷺ, during his Khilaafat, requesting a short advice. Hadhrat Aisha ﷺ wrote in reply,

"Peace be upon you! I heard Rasulullaah ﷺ say that whoever remains indifferent to the anger of people in his obedience to Allaah, Allaah Ta'ala will safeguard him from the effects of their anger and whoever will anger Allaah to please people then Allaah Ta'ala will destroy him at the hands of those very people."[1]

[1] 'Tirmidhi'

The radiance of his blessed face

Hadhrat Aisha ؓ narrates that she had borrowed a needle from Hadhrat Hafsah binte Ruwaahah ؓ, with which she used to patch the clothes of Rasulullaah ﷺ.

One night the needle fell from her hands and after searching for it for a long time could not find it on account of the darkness. Just then Rasulullaah ﷺ entered the house and as he entered the entire house was lit up by the radiance from his blessed face, such that Hadhrat Aisha ؓ was able to see the needle. With a huge smile on her face Hadhrat Aisha ؓ picked up the needle.[1]

[1]'Kanzul Ummaal'

Hadhrat Aisha's assistance to all women

Some guardians forcefully perform the marriage of their daughters without their consent. During the era of Rasulullaah ﷺ a few incidents of this sort also transpired. Hadhrat Aisha ﷺ was the representative of woman in that era. A woman whose Nikaah had been performed forcefully came to see Rasulullaah ﷺ but he was not home at that time.

The woman narrated he plight to Hadhrat Aisha ﷺ that her father has forced her to marry his nephew, in order to elevate his status in society, even though she was unhappy with the union.

Hadhrat Aisha ﷺ advised the woman to explain her entire condition to Rasulullaah ﷺ when he arrives, which she subsequently did. Rasulullaah ﷺ summoned her father and granted her the choice to annul the marriage. She replied, "O Rasulullaah ﷺ! I will abide by the decision of my father. My intention was only to make known to women the rights thatthey have."[1]

[1]'Nasaai'

Defending Hadhrat Ali ﵁

When Hadhrat Ali ﵁ was martyred by the Khawaarij and people came and related the tale of his martyrdom to her she asked one of them, "I wish to ask you something but answer me honestly." He replied that he would most definitely do so.

Hadhrat Aisha ﵂ enquired about the state of those people who had martyred Hadhrat Ali﵁. He replied, "They are those who opposed the agreement between Hadhrat Ali ﵁ and Hadhrat Muawiyah ﵁." He then related the manner in which Hadhrat Ali ﵁ tied to make them understand and how they refused to accept his explanation. On hearing this Hadhrat Aisha ﵂ said, "May Allaah Ta'ala have mercy on Ali ﵁. Whenever anything was to his liking he would say, "Allaah and His Rasul have spoken the truth". **The people of Iraq wrongfully accuse him, inflating matters before relating it."**[1]

[1]'Musnad Ahmed', 'Bukhaari'

Abstinence and self-denial

Hadhrat Aisha ﵂ was blessed with the admirable quality of contentment. The manner in which she spent her married life; under difficult conditions of poverty and hardship, is not hidden from anybody. However despite these harsh conditions she never once complained. She did not receive any exquisite clothing, priceless jewels, enormous palaces or any other worldly adornment from her husband, Rasulullaah ﷺ. She even witnessed the wealth of the world flowing into Madinah from the many conquests of the Muslims but never sought it or even desired it.

Once after the demise of Rasulullaah ﷺ she asked for some food to be brought to her, on which she said that she never eats to her full. One of her students, who would come to her every day, asked her the reason for that. Hadhrat Aisha ﵂ replied, "I remember the condition when Rasulullaah ﷺ left this world. I take an oath by Allaah! **Rasulullaah ﷺ never ate two meals of bread and meat in a day, eating to his full.**[1]

[1]'Tirmidhi'

An amazing manner of showing anger

Hadhrat Aisha ﵂ always abstained from belittling or speaking ill of someone and in fact it has never been reported that she ever slandered anyone. She would speak only good of the other wives of Rasulullaah ﷺ as well. Hadhrat Hassaan ﵁ who was also caught in the false accusation against Hadhrat Aisha ﵂ was never spoken ill of or even run down by her. In fact Hadhrat Hassaan ﵁ would sit in her discourses and she would allow him to as well.

On one occasion Hadhrat Hassaan bin Thaabit ﵁came to Hadhrat Aisha ﵂ ad related one of his poems to her, in which one line meant, "He does not falsely accuse innocent woman". On hearing this Hadhrat Aisha ﵂ was reminded of the incident of 'Ifq' but did not say anything to him except, "But you are not like that."[1]

[1]'Seerat Aisha'

Abstinence from slander

In a similar manner once, some of her family were discussing the sad events of how Hadhrat Aisha ﵂ was falsely accused and on account of Hadhrat Hassaan's ﵁ involvement began to speak ill of him. Hadhrat Aisha ﵂ was present and immediately said to them angrily, "Do not speak ill of Hassaan﵁, as he would defend Rasulullaah ﷺ from the poetry of the Mushrikeen."[1]

[1] 'Seerat Aisha'

Compassion for the entire world

Once a woman came to beg from Hadhrat Aisha ﵂ accompanied by her two infant children. Hadhrat Aisha ﵂ only had three dates with her and gave them to the woman. The woman gave a date to each of her children and placed the other in her mouth. The children quickly consumed the date they were given and looked longingly at their mother. When the mother saw her children staring at her, she took the date out of her mouth and after dividing it in half gave it to her children to eat. Seeing the love of the mother for her children and their sad plight, Hadhrat Aisha ﵂ began to weep.

An amazing punishment

On one occasion Hadhrat Aisha ﵂ fell ill and people suggested that perhaps it could be the result of black magic. Hadhrat Aisha ﵂ summoned her servant and asked her if she was responsible. The servant confessed and when asked the reason for doing so she replied, "So that you can leave this world quickly and I may be set free." As punishment for her crime, (which should have been death for attempting to take the life of the blessed wife of Rasulullaah ﷺ), Hadhrat Aisha ﵂ ordered that she should be sold to a firm individual and with the money receive another slave be bought and set free. This is exactly what was done and another slave was purchased and set free.[1]

[1]'Daar Quthni', 'Muwatta Imaam Maalik', 'Mustadrak Haakim'

An excellent example of good relations

On one occasion Hadhrat Aisha was washing her hands when Rasulullaah passed by. Hadhrat Aisha lovingly sprinkled some water on him. Rasulullaah also immediately took a handful of water and splashed Hadhrat Aisha. Rasulullaah then said, "O Aisha! I did not overstep but only retaliated and permissibility to retaliate is in the Quraan."[1]

[1] ibid

Reminding the other wives of Rasulullaah ﷺ about his decree

After the demise of Rasulullaah ﷺ, the blessed wives of Rasulullaah ﷺ sent Hadhrat Uthmaan ﵁ to the Khalifah Hadhrat Abu Bakr ﵁ seeking their share of the inheritance. Hadhrat Aisha ﵂ narrates that she prohibited the wives of Rasulullaah ﷺ from making this demand saying to them, "Do you not fear Allaah? Are you not aware that Rasulullaah ﷺ said, "There is no inheritance in my wealth, whatever I leave behind is Sadaqah." When the blessed wives of Rasulullaah ﷺ were reminded of this they all abstained from these demands.[1]

[1]'Bukhaari', 'Muwatta Imaam Muhammed'

Hadhrat Aisha's learns of punishment of the grave

On one occasion two Jewish women came to Hadhrat Aisha and in the conversation that ensued they said to her, "May Allaah save you from the punishment of the grave." This was something new to Hadhrat Aisha and she said to them that punishment will not occur in the grave. In doubt over the matter, when Rasulullaah arrived she enquired as to whether there will be punishment in the grave. Rasulullaah then informed her that there would be punishment in the grave.[1]

Thereafter Hadhrat Aisha when listening to the supplication of Rasulullaah closely found that he sought protection from the punishment in the grave.

[1]'Bukhaari'

He taught the world the principle of life

Hadhrat Aisha narrates that an old woman came to see Rasulullaah and Rasulullaah enquired who she was. She relied that her name was Jathaamah Mazaniyah. Rasulullaah replied to her, "No! As from today your name will be Husaanah Mazaniyah." Rasulullaah then enquired about her well-being and how she has been keeping. She replied, "O Rasulullaah! We are in good condition, may my parents be sacrificed for you."

Later after she left Hadhrat Aisha asked, "O Rasulullaah! You showed such gracious treatment to that old woman (what was the reason for this?)" **Rasulullaah replied, "She was the friend of Hadhrat Khadijah, who used to visit us frequently and to maintain old relations is a part of Imaan."**[1]

[1] 'Baihaqi'

Testifying to the truth before the governor, Marwaan

Marwaan bin Hakam was the governor of Madinah and he announced the Khilaafat of Yazeed in a public gathering. Hadhrat Abdur Rahmaan bin Abu Bakr, the brother of Hadhrat Aisha opposed this announcement. Marwaan was angered by this and intended to arrest him but Hadhrat Abdur Rahmaan took refuge in the home of Hadhrat Aisha. Marwaan bin Hakam did not have the courage to enter the home of Hadhrat Aisha and standing outside he shouted loudly, "He is the same person regarding whom the verse was revealed, "And do not utter "Oof" unto them."

On hearing this Hadhrat Aisha called out from behind the veil, "Allaah Ta'ala did not reveal any verse regarding us (the family of Hadhrat Abu Bakr) except regarding my innocence."[1]

One can gauge from this that Hadhrat Aisha was also not pleased at the appointment of Yazeed as Khalifah.[2]

---

[1] 'Bukhaari'
[2] 'Seerat Aisha'

Is it permissible to retaliate

On one occasion Rasulullaah ﷺ once threw a stick playfully towards Hadhrat Aisha ﵂ which inadvertently struck her leg. Hadhrat Aisha ﵂ smiled at Rasulullaah ﷺ and said, "O Rasulullaah ﷺ! Is it permissible to retaliate?" Rasulullaah ﷺ understood that she had been hurt by the stick and said, "It is permissible to retaliate but not when it was a mistake."[1]

[1]'Mustadrak Haakim'

Recompense on killing snake

Once Hadhrat Aisha ﷺ saw a snake in the house, which she killed. Later someone told her that she should not have done that because it is possible that this could have been a Muslim Jinn. Hadhrat Aisha ﷺ replied that if it was a Muslim Jinn then it would not have entered the house of Ummul Mu'mineen." The person replied, "You were veiled when he entered." Hadhrat Aisha ﷺ was so affected by this person's argument that she set one slave free in recompense for killing the snake.[1]

[1]'Musnad Ahmed'

Resolving disputes

Rasulullaah ﷺ always maintained good relations with his wives, always cheering them up. Hadhrat Aisha رضي الله عنها narrates that whenever she would have an argument with Rasulullaah ﷺ then Rasulullaah ﷺ would try to console her. If she did not resolve the matter then Rasulullaah ﷺ would suggest getting someone to act as mediator in the matter.

On one occasions this is exactly what occurred and Rasulullaah ﷺ suggested, "If you agree then we should get Hadhrat Umar رضي الله عنه to act as mediator." Hadhrat Aisha رضي الله عنها replied, "No! Umar رضي الله عنه is too strict. I will appoint my father as mediator." Hadhrat Abu Bakr رضي الله عنه arrived and after hearing the situation began to hit Hadhrat Aisha رضي الله عنها. She immediately stood and hid behind Rasulullaah ﷺ.

Hadhrat Aisha narrates, "When my father left then I separated myself from Rasulullaah and sat in the corner. Rasulullaah called me but I refused to go to him. Rasulullaah ﷺ then laughed and said, "A few moments ago you were hiding behind me and now you refuse to come to me."[1]

[1]'Seerat Aisha'

Three things

Hadhrat Aisha asked, "O Rasulullaah! What are those things which are impermissible to deny one who asks for it?" Rasulullaah replied, "Water, salt and fire." Hadhrat Aisha asked, "I understand water but what is the reason for not refusing salt and fire."Rasulullaah replied, O Humairah! Whoever gives a person fire then whatever is cooked using it, it is as if it has all been donated to Allaah and whoever gives a person salt then whatever increase in taste it creates, then it is as if it all has been donated to Allaah Ta'ala. If a person gives a Muslim water to drink where water is available then it is as if he has set a slave free and if he gives a Muslims water to drink where there is no water available then it is as if he given life to that thirsty person."[1]

[1]'Ibn Maajah'

That which gives beauty

On one occasion Hadhrat Aisha رضي الله عنها accompanied Rasulullaah ﷺ on a journey. The camel Hadhrat Aisha رضي الله عنها was riding upon was extremely stubborn and would sometimes pull to the left and at others to the right. Seeing this Rasulullaah ﷺ said, "O Aisha! Be soft and gentle. Verily these are such qualities that it become a means of beauty in those who possess it and seen as a fault in those who are deprived of it."[1]

[1] 'Seerat Aisha'

A supplication for fever

Hadhrat Anas ؓ narrates that Rasulullaah ﷺ once came to Hadhrat Aisha ؓ and she had fever, which she was complaining of. Rasulullaah ﷺ replied, "Do not complain of the fever as it has been ordered by Allaah Ta'ala. However if you so wish then I will teach you such a supplication through which Allaah Ta'ala will grant you cure. When Hadhrat Aisha ؓ asked to be taught the supplication Rasulullaah ﷺ said,

اَللّٰھُمَّ ارحم جلد الرقيق و عظم الدقيق من شدة الحريق يا ام ملام ان كنت امنت بالله العلى يعلم فلا تصدعى الرئس و ال تتنى الضم و لاتئكلى اللحم و لا تشر الدم و تحولى عنى انى من اتخف مع الله اله اخر

O Allaah! Have mercy upon my thin skin and weak bones, and protect me from the intensity of the heat. O Ummul Malaam! (the name given to fever) I seek refuge in Allaah the Most High to safeguard me from you creating pain in my head and odour in my mouth. Do not consume my flesh nor my blood. Leave me and go to those who call unto other deities besides Allaah."[1]

---

[1]'Baihaqi'

Rasulullaah's ﷺ bedding

Hadhrat Aisha ﷺ narrates that a woman of the Ansaar came to visit her and she saw the bedding of Rasulullaah ﷺ which consisted of a folded sheet. Later she sent a bedding that was filled with wool.

When Rasulullaah ﷺ returned he enquired as to what it was, Hadhrat Aisha replied, "O Rasulullaah ﷺ! A woman from the Ansaar came to me and after seeing your bedding, she left. She later sent me this bedding for you." On hearing this Rasulullaah ﷺ said three times, "Return it! Return it! Return it! I like the old bedding that I used to have." Hadhrat Aisha ﷺ replied that she wanted to keep it but Rasulullaah ﷺ insisted that she return it saying, "Return it! For I take an oath by Allaah if I so desired My Rabb would let mountains of gold and silver follow me."[1]

[1]'Baihaqi, 'Ibn Sa'ad', 'Khasa'is Kubra'

No oil in the house

Hadhrat Aisha ﵂ narrates that Hadhrat Abu Bakr ﵁ once sent them a leg of a sheep, which she held and Rasulullaah ﷺ cut or Rasulullaah ﷺ held and she cut. The narrator says that he asked Hadhrat Aisha ﵂, "Did this take place under the light of the lamp?" Hadhrat Aisha ﵂ replied, "If we had oil to light the lamp we would have rather consumed it."[1]

[1]'Tabraani'

Dislike for praise

Hadhrat Aisha ﵂ had taken seriously ill before her demise. People flocked from across the empire to visit her and others to treat her. Whenever any person would ask how she felt, she would reply that she is feeling well and whenever any person would praise her then she would say, "If only I would be turned into a lifeless rock."

On one occasion Hadhrat Abdullaah bin Abbaas ﵄ came to visit her and sought permission to enter, Hadhrat Aisha ﵂ had second thoughts of allowing him to enter as she knew that he would praise her. However her nephews intercede for him, saying that he was amongst his pious and good sons and she reluctantly permitted him to enter.

Hadhrat Abdullaah in Abbaas ﵄ entered and said, "Your title has been Ummul Mu'mineen from eternity, you are the most beloved of all Rasulullaah's ﷺ wives. You now only have to wait for that amount of time to be reunited with Rasulullaah ﷺ and your family that it would take for your soul to leave your body. You were the most beloved of all the blessed wives of Rasulullaah ﷺ according to him and Rasulullaah ﷺonly loved that which was pure. Your necklace was lost on the night of Abwa and Rasulullaah ﷺ and all people encamped (to look for it), when there was no water Allaah Ta'ala revealed the verse, "Perform Tayammum with clean soil". You were the reason for such ease to be revealed to the Ummat. Allaah Ta'ala revealed verses in the Noble Quraan enumerating your excellence."

Hadhrat Aisha ﵂ replied to him, "Ibn Abbaas! Excuse me from such praise.I desire that I be forgotten."[1]

[1]'Bukhaari', 'Mustadrak Haakim'

Preference given to Hadhrat Umar

It was the desire of Hadhrat Umar ﷺ to also be buried alongside Rasulullaah ﷺ in the house of Hadhrat Aisha ﷺ but out of respect for Hadhrat Aisha ﷺ could not ask her permission.

In the last moments of his life, he was still restless with this desire and finally asked his son to seek permission from Hadhrat Aisha ﷺ on his behalf. He ordered him to pass on his Salaams and say, "It is desire of Umar to be buried alongside his friends."

Hadhrat Abdullaah bin Umar ﷺ went to Hadhrat Aisha ﷺ and related the entire conversation to her and she replied, "even though I had been reserving that place for myself but I am willing to give preference to Umar ﷺ over myself. Bury him in my room on the alongside Rasulullaah ﷺ."

Hadhrat Umar ﷺ was informed that Hadhrat Aisha ﷺ had granted him permission but he still made a bequest that after he passes away, his Janaazah should be taken to the resting place of Rasulullaah ﷺ and then permission again sought from Hadhrat Aisha ﷺ. If she grants permission then only enter and bury me there but if she does not give permission then bury me in the graveyard of the Muslims."

They acted in accordance with his wishes, seeking permission again and Hadhrat Aisha once again granted her permission and then only was Hadhrat Umar buried alongside Rasulullaah.

To Allaah do we belong and unto Him shall we return

Hadhrat Aisha passed away towards the end of the Khilaafat of Hadhrat Muawiyah. She was 67 years old. She fell ill in Ramadaan 85 A.H and after a few days on 17 Ramadaan, 13 June 678 C.E she left this earthly abode. *To Allaah do we belong and unto Him shall we return.*

She made a bequest before passing away to be buried alongside the other blessed wives of Rasulullaah in Jannatul Baqee'a. She asked to be buried immediately after her death without any delay. **Her wishes were fulfilled and she was buried in the cover of night in Jannatul Baqee'a.** There was such a large crowd for her Janaazah that it has been said that there was never such a huge gathering for a Janaazah at night prior to this. Some have mentioned that due to the large number of women present one could have mistaken it to have been Eid Salaah.

Hadhrat Abu Hurairah was the acting governor of Madinah and he performed the Janaazah. Qaasim bin Muhammed, Abdullaah bin Abdur Rahmaan, Abdullaah bin Ateeq, Urwah bin Zubair, and Abdullaah bin Zubair lowered her into her grave.[1]

[1]'Bukhaari'

	Name of book	Name of Author
1	Noble Quraan	
2	Ruhul Bayaan	Allaamah Abu Fadhl Shahaabudeen Sayyid Mahmood Aaloosi (127 A.H)
3	Tafseerul Kabeer	Imaam Fakhrudien Raazi (606 A.H)
4	Tafseer Ibn Katheer	Imaam Imaadudien Abul Fidaa Isma'eel bin Katheer Qurashi (774 A.H)
5	Tafseerul Khaazin	Allaamah Alaa'udeen Ali bin Muhammed Baghdadi Al-Khaazin (725 A.H)
6	TafseerMa'aariful Quraan	Allaamah Mufti Muhammed Shafie Uthmaani
7	Bukhaari	Imaam Muhammed bin Isma'eel Bukhaari (256 A.H)
8	Muslim	Imaam Muslim bin Hajjaaj Al-Qushairi Nisapoori (251 A.H)
9	Tirmidhi	Imaam Abu Isa Muhammed bin Isa Tirmidhi (279 A.H)
10	Abu Dawood	Imaam Abu Dawood Sulaimaan bin Ash'ath Sijistaani (275 A.H)
11	Nasaai	Imaam Abu Abdur Rahmaan Ahmed bin Shuaib Nasaai (303 A.H)
12	Ibn Maajah	Imaam Abu Abdullaah Muhammed bin Yazeed Qazweeni (273 A.H)
13	Daarmie	Imaam Abdullaah bin Abdur Rahmaan Daarmie (255 A.H)
14	Musnad Ahmed	Imaam Ahmed bin Hanbal
15	Muwatta Imaam Maalik	Imaam Maalik bin Anas Madani (179 A.H)
16	Muwatta Imaam Muhammed	Imaam Muhammed bin Hasan Shaybaani (189 A.H)
17	Shamaail Tirmidhi	Imaam Abu Isa Muhammed bin Isa Tirmidhi (279 A.H)
18	Mishkaatul Masaabeeh	Imaam Abu Abdullaah Muhammedbin Abdullaah Al-Khateeb
19	Kanzul Ummaal	Allaamah Alaa'udeen Ali Al-Muttaqi
20	Fathul Baarie	Imaam Ahmed bin Ali bin Hajar Askalaani (852 A.H)
21	As-Sharah Lil Imaam Nawawi	Imaam Abu Zakariyya Yahya bin Sharh Nawawi

22	Tuhfatul Ahwathi	Moulana Abdur Rahmaan Mubarakpuri
23	Al-Urfush Shadhi	Allaamah Muhammed Anwar Shah Kashmiri
24	Kashful Baarie	Sheikhul Hadeeth Allaamah Saleemullah Khan sahib
25	Haashia Sindhi	Imaam Abul Hasan Sindhi
26	Al-Bidaayah wan Nihaayah	Allaamah Ibn Katheer
27	Seerat Aisha	Allaamah Sayyid Sulaimaan Nadwi
28	Hayaatus Sahabah	Allaamah Muhammed Yusuf Khandhlawi
29	Qasas Ma'aariful Quraan	Allaamah Mufti Muhammed Shafie Uthmaani

Translation edited by
A.H.Elias (Mufti)
May Allaah protect him
3rd Ramadhaan 1433
23 th July 2012

An Nabi al Khaatam

The Seal of the Ambiyaa-Messengers

By:

Maulana Manaazir Ahsan Gilani

Translation Edited By:

Mufti Afzal Hoosen Elias

(May Allaah Protect him)

ZAM ZAM
PUBLISHERS

100 Stories
of
Hadhrat Faatimah رضي الله عنها

By:
Moulana Muhammed Uwais Saror

Translation Edited By:
Mufti Afzal Hoosen Elias
(May Allaah Protect him)

ZAM ZAM
PUBLISHERS

NOTE